GREAT BRITAIN AND IRELAND

THE ENGLISH-SPEAKING WORLD

Join the Team

ANGLAIS 6e

Édition 2010

A1 → A2

Sous la direction de

Hélène Adrian
IA – IPR
Académie de Versailles

Cyril Dowling
Professeur agrégé
Lycée français de Barcelone
Conseiller pédagogique

Sylvain Kustyan
Professeur certifié
Collège Blaise Pascal, Mazingarbe (62)
Formateur associé – Académie de Lille

Sylvie Sandra
Professeur certifié
Collège Vauban, Maubeuge (59)
Formatrice associée – Académie de Lille

Eric Tian-Sio-Po
Professeur certifié
Collège Honoré de Balzac, Albi (81)
Académie de Toulouse

Nathan

En fin de 6e, l'objectif est de confirmer le niveau A1 et d'amorcer le niveau A2.

	Écouter	Lire	Prendre part à une conversation	S'exprimer orlement en continu	Écrire
A1	Comprendre des mots familiers et des expressions courantes.	Comprendre des mots familiers, ainsi que des phrases très simples, par exemple des annonces, des affiches ou des catalogues.	Communiquer de façon simple, à condition que l'interlocuteur soit disposé à répéter ou à reformuler ses phrases plus lentement et à aider à formuler ce que l'on essaie de dire. Poser des questions simples sur des sujets familiers ou sur ce dont on a imédiatement besoin. Répondre à de telles questions.	Utiliser des expressions et des phrases simples pour décrire son lieu d'habitation et les gens que l'on connaît.	Écrire une courte carte postale simple, par exemple de vacances. Remplir un questionnaire : par exemple inscrire son nom, sa nationalité et son adresse sur une fiche d'hôtel.
A2-1	Reconnaître des énoncés simples déjà rencontrés et entendus dans des situations familières. Comprendre les nombres et les chiffres isolés ainsi que des mots simples désignant des personnages dans un récit très bref.	Comprendre à l'écrit des énoncés déjà rencontrés auparavant. Repérer les thèmes essentiels abordés dans un courrier personnel ou dans un texte traitant d'un domaine familier.	Prendre part à des conversations brèves dans des situations simples et habituelles (rencontre, achats, demande de renseignements) sans que l'interlocuteur manifeste de grandes difficultés pour comprendre.	Se présenter ainsi que sa famille et ses amis (identité, travail, loisirs, domicile) en quelques phrases simples.	Transcrire en 2 ou 3 phrases une information simple communiquée oralement.

Édition : Fanny Husson, Fanny Blanchard
Illustrations : Laurent Audouin, Philippe Gady (p. 62,116), Bruno Liance, Sébastien Telleschi, Maureen Wingrove
Iconographie : Valérie Delchambre
Conception de la maquette : Frédéric Jely
Couverture : Grégoire Bourdin
Cartographie : Légendes Cartographie
Mise en pages : Anne-Danielle Naname, Adeline Calame

ISBN 978-2-09-173815-4

Avant-propos

La nouvelle édition 2010 de Join the Team 6e entend à la fois conserver les points forts de l'édition de 2006 tout en prenant en compte les nouveaux besoins nés de l'évolution des pratiques des quatre dernières années.

Elle intègre de nouveaux médias (audio, vidéo, Internet, multimédia) qui vous permettront de profiter de tous les atouts du numérique.

Le manuel contient 7 parties contenant 2 à 3 unités, soit un total de 16 unités suffisamment courtes pour pouvoir mener à bien la découverte de l'ensemble du programme durant l'année de sixième.

Professeurs et élèves retrouveront dans cette nouvelle édition la prise en compte :

- du lien entre école primaire et collège,
- des différents types d'activités langagières (compréhension écrite et orale, expression écrite et orale),
- des différents outils de la langue,
- de la dimension culturelle qui constitue certes un objectif en elle-même, mais sert avant tout de fil conducteur et fournit la thématique des différentes unités,
- et enfin, des stratégies qui peuvent offrir une aide conséquente aux élèves, tant en compréhension qu'en production, dans la rubrique ***Tactics***.

Le manuel entend apporter un juste équilibre entre acquisition et maîtrise des outils, d'une part, et l'intégration de ces outils dans de réelles activités de communication d'autre part.

Ce manuel fait la part belle à un travail systématique visant l'acquisition des outils dans les pages ***Discover*** notamment, qui sont ensuite aussitôt réinvestis dans un travail d'entraînement au sein d'une activité langagière.

Un grand nombre d'exercices est offert à cette fin dans le manuel (***Grammar***, ***English lab***, ***Language practice***), dans le Workbook et dans le CD-ROM élève.

L'accent est mis sur le lexique, en particulier sur la découverte et la mémorisation d'un vocabulaire d'une grande cohérence thématique.

On trouvera aussi dans le manuel de nombreuses activités de communication contextualisées ***Your task*** à la mesure des élèves en termes d'âge et d'acquis langagiers.

Enfin, les élèves sont pleinement impliqués dans les activités d'auto-évaluation du manuel (***Check your progress***) et du Workbook (***Quick check***) qui leur permettent de se situer plus finement dans leur parcours de **A1- à A2-**, le niveau A2 constituant l'objectif visé en fin de cinquième.

Nous souhaitons à chaque élève et à chaque professeur de trouver plaisir à travailler avec ce manuel résolument moderne !

Les auteurs

Présentation du manuel

Les logos utilisés dans le manuel

- Écouter
- Lire
- Parler en continu
- Parler en interaction
- Écrire

- PISTE 00 — Document enregistré sur le CD audio-rom élève
- Document enregistré sur les CD classe
- Audio-Rom — Exercices disponibles sur le CD audio-rom élève
- DVD — Document à visionner sur le DVD

- → Go to your WB p. 00 — Renvoi au Workbook
- Wordgym → Go to your WB p. 00 — Renvoi à une activité de lexique dans le Workbook
- QUICK CHECK → WB p. 00 — Renvoi à une activité d'auto-évaluation dans le Workbook

En début de manuel

Welcome : une partie de transition primaire – collège

La structure d'une partie

Deux ou trois unités par partie

Ouverture de partie

- Une chanson pour entrer dans la thématique de l'unité
- Les tâches intermédiaires (une par unité)
- La tâche finale de l'unité

Part 2

Home, sweet home

A mouse in my house

A new friend, a new buddy,
I've got a little mouse in my study.
He's got a red hat,
He loves my old cat,
And in the kitchen, he plays with the kitten.
He likes cake, he likes jelly,
He likes candy bars dipped in honey!
But he doesn't like cheese! 'Coz it makes him sneeze!
He doesn't like bread! It makes his nose red!

Chorus
Oh yes I'm happy! I know I'm lucky!
I've got a little mouse in my house! (…)

Unit 3 YOUR TASK Write a short note for the school magazine about your favourite star's bedroom ... p. 36

Unit 4 YOUR TASK Write a poem about your favourite food ... p. 42

FINAL TASK Create a hero for a TV series. Describe his/her lifestyle. ... p. 47

Ouverture d'unité

- Un grand visuel pour entrer dans la thématique de l'unité
- Les objectifs d'apprentissage par activité langagière
- Les outils de la langue à maîtriser

Discover

une page de découverte des outils de langue

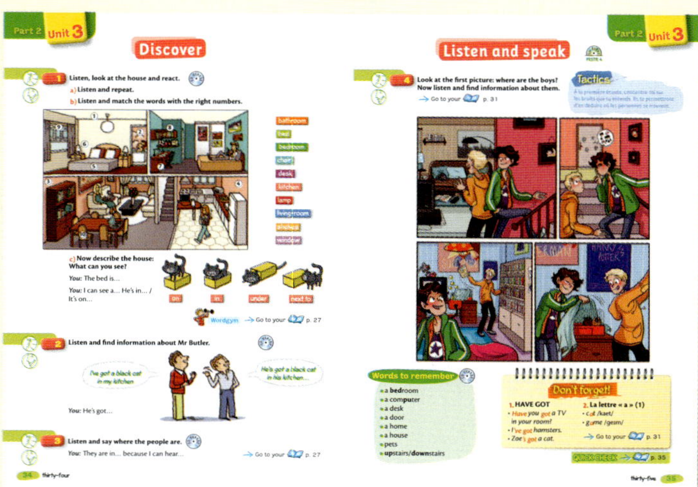

Un document oral **Listen and speak** ou écrit **Read and Speak** pour acquérir les outils de langue

Use what you know

une page d'activités de transfert

- ***Speak for a minute*** prise de parole en continu
- ***Write a few lines*** rédaction
- ***Speak in pairs*** interaction orale
- ***Your task*** tâches intermédiaires

Grammar

- les points de langue vus dans l'unité et des exercices
- l'***English Lab*** pour s'entraîner à la prononciation de l'anglais

Les rubriques récurrentes

Video Flash
Extraits vidéo authentiques

Tactics
Conseils méthodologiques

Don't forget!
Grammaire et phonologie de la leçon

Words to remember
Outils lexicaux

Did you know?
Zoom sur un point culturel

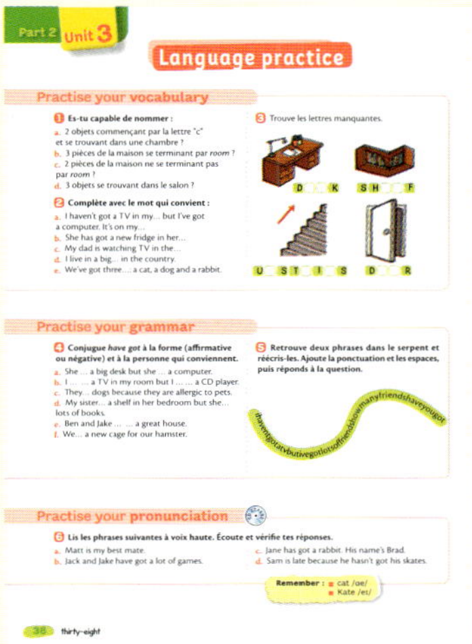

Language practice

une page d'exercices ludiques de grammaire, de lexique et de prononciation

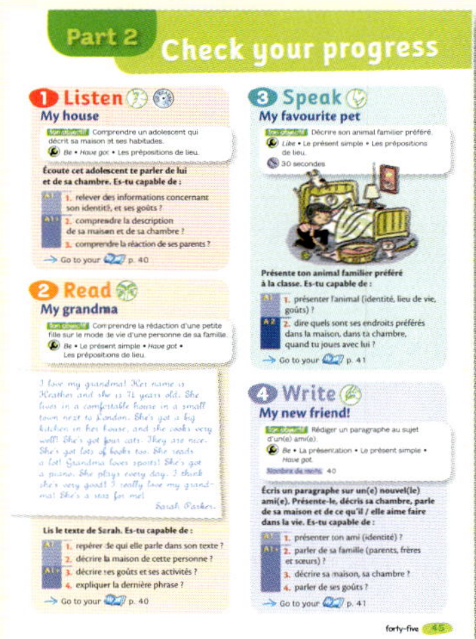

Check your progress

Des activités d'auto-évaluation par activités langagières

Discovery

- 2 pages de documents pour découvrir le monde anglophone
- ***Quiz Time*** : des activités de compréhension
- ***Final task*** : une tâche finale, concrète et ludique
- Des pistes de recherche sur Internet

En fin de manuel

- 8 pages ***British Festivities***
- 2 pages ***Read***
- Les scripts des ***Listen and Speak***
- ***Exercise bank***: les exercices supplémentaires de grammaire et de vocabulaire du CD-Rom de l'élève
- **Un test d'évaluation**
- **Un précis grammatical**
- Un **lexique** anglais-français et français-anglais

Sommaire

Welcome

Show what you know

**Pour faire le point sur ce que tu connais déjà en anglais, voici 6 défis.
À toi de les relever !**

Challenge 1 Meet a new friend

**Ton nouveau correspondant t'a envoyé un message.
Écoute-le et note les informations que tu as repérées en t'aidant des illustrations.**

→ Go to your WB p. 4

Challenge 2 Meet the family

**Ton correspondant t'a envoyé une photo de ses frères.
Écoute attentivement et associe chaque personnage aux prénoms suivants : Tom, Jack, Patrick, Rick.**

→ Go to your WB p. 4

1 2 3 4

Challenge 3 Get in touch

Tu viens de recevoir un e-mail de ton correspondant. Quelle réponse vas-tu lui faire ?

Hello! I'm your new penfriend. I live in London. I hope you're ok. My new school is great. I like my new teachers especially my French teacher.
Please write soon!
Love from Sam.

a) Recopie son e-mail.

b) Réponds-lui en te servant des phrases de ton correspondant pour te presenter brièvement.

→ Go to your WB p. 4

Challenge 4 A great visit

Ton correspondant américain t'a envoyé ce prospectus. Il a beaucoup aimé la visite qu'il a faite. Lis-le attentivement et explique de quoi il s'agit.

→ Go to your WB p. 5

Come and visit the best zoo on the planet!

800 SPECIES! 4,000 ANIMALS!
1 MILLION PLANTS!

A great experience for adults and children! MARCH – OCTOBER
Everyday from 9 a.m. to 9 p.m.

NOVEMBER – FEBRUARY
From Tuesday to Sunday 10 a.m. to 7 p.m.

Prices:
- Adult (+12): $35
- Child (3-11): $26
- Child (under 3): Free

Challenge 5 What's your favourite food?

Interroge un de tes camarades pour qu'il (elle) réponde aux questions du formulaire.

Name:

Age:

City:

Favourite food:

Use: Ice cream vegetables meat

→ Go to your WB p. 5

Challenge 6 Spot the differences

Regarde attentivement les deux illustrations et repère au moins 5 différences.
Fais cinq phrases pour les décrire.

You: In picture 1, it's snowing but in picture 2, the sun is shining.

1

2

→ Go to your WB p. 5

Nice to meet you!

Tu vas maintenant faire la connaissance des personnages de ton livre. Écoute-les et présente-toi à ton tour.

1. Listen to Chad and say who you are

a) Listen to Chad and answer his question.

b) Listen and sing the alphabet song.

**c) Play a memory game with your classmates.
Listen and choose an English name.**

Andrew	Ben	Edward	Steven	Allan	Dan	Sean
Brad	David	Michael	Bruce	Laura	Linda	Eileen
Fiona	Samantha	Sue	Phoebe	Mary	Liza	Kate

d) Now play the name spelling game.

Pupil A: What's your name?
Pupil B: I'm Steven S-T-E-V-E-N.
Pupil A: I'm Edward E-D-W-A-R-D and this is Steven, S-T-E-V-E-N.
Pupil B: What's your name?
Pupil C: I'm Kate, K-A-T-E.
Pupil B: I'm Steven, this is Edward, E-D-W-A-R-D and this is Kate, K-A-T-E.

→ Go to your WB p. 6

2. Listen to Tom and say your age

a) Listen to Tom and answer his question.

b) Now let's count up to 90: listen and repeat.

→ Go to your WB p. 6

1	2	3	4	5	6	7	8	9	10	11
one	two	three	four	five	six	seven	eight	nine	ten	eleven

12	13	14	15	16	17	18	19
twelve	thirteen	fourteen	fifteen	sixteen	seventeen	eighteen	nineteen

20	30	40	50	60	70	80	90
twenty	thirty	forty	fifty	sixty	seventy	eighty	ninety

3. Listen to Mrs Monroe and say where you live

CD CLASSE

a) Listen to Mrs Monroe and answer her question.

Countries	Nationalities
Republic of Ireland	Irish
England	English
Wales	Welsh
The United Kingdom	British
Scotland	Scottish

b) Match names and nationalities. → Go to your WB p. 7

4. Listen to Zoe and say what you like

CD CLASSE

a) Listen to Zoe and answer her question.

b) Now read the poem and list the different colours.

Blue is the sea

Blue is the sea,
Green is the grass,
White are the clouds
As they slowly pass.

Black are the crows,
Brown are the trees,
Red are the sails
Of a ship in the breeze.

→ Go to your WB p. 7

YOUR TASK

Play the spy game

1. Imagine a new identity: name, age, nationality, country, telephone number...
2. Ask your classmate questions to discover his/her new identity. Answer his or her questions about your identity.

→ Go to your WB p. 7

Name : ....
Age : ....
City : ....
Country : ....

School time

Tu vas maintenant entrer dans l'univers d'une école anglaise. Découvre quelques situations de classe et apprends à réagir en anglais.

1. Good morning, Miss!

CD CLASSE

a) Look at the pictures and listen.

b) Match the pictures with the sentences.

2. Have you got your book?

CD CLASSE

a) Listen to the words. Match the words with the right numbers.

Remember!
What's that? It's a book
It's an eraser.

b) Listen to Tom. What has he got in his school bag?

→ Go to your WB p. 8

c) And you, what have you got in your school bag today?
You: I've got… but I…

3. Listen to your teacher!

a) Listen to the teacher and match the sentences with the pictures.

b) Now listen again and repeat.

Go to your WB p. 8

4. What's the day, today?

a) Listen, repeat and recite the poem. Then, answer the questions.
You: Today is...

Every week has 7 days,
See how many you can say.
Sunday, Monday, Tuesday,
Wednesday, Thursday, Friday,
Saturday. What's today?

Go to your WB p. 8

b) Listen and match the month with the season.

5. What time is it?

a) Listen and say if it's in the morning or in the afternoon.

b) Listen and complete the clocks.

Go to your WB p. 9

YOUR TASK

Pretend you are the teacher

1. **Welcome the class.**
2. **Do the registration: ask who is missing and complete a form.**
3. **Ask if the pupils are ready (books, pens, ruler...).**
4. **Give them instructions.**

Go to your WB p. 9

Part 1 School friends

Welcome to my school!

CD ÉLÈVE PISTE 1 Karaoké

Welcome to my school!
Come in, and be cool!
Good morning, you can all sit down!
I'm Mister Parker
Yes, I'm your teacher
Good morning, Good morning Sir!

Can you repeat? I think I don't know
I don't understand... Can I open the window?
Can you come to the board? Can you write the date?
Yes sir! Yes sir! It's a piece of cake!

Welcome to my school!
Let's all be cheerful!
Take your pens and write this down
I'm Mister Parker!
Listen to your teacher!
Yes Sir! No Sir! Thank you Sir! (...)

Unit 1 Back to school

Je vais m'entraîner à

- Comprendre des informations sur une école. Comprendre des informations sur l'identité de quelqu'un.
- Comprendre un e-mail.
- Présenter un ou une ami(e).
- Me renseigner sur l'identité de quelqu'un.
- Présenter son école et ses professeurs.

Je vais utiliser

Be au présent................ p. 21

Les questions................ p. 21

Le lexique de l'école (1).

→ Go to your WB p. 10

Discover

1 **Look at the drawing.**

a) Who and what can you see? Where is it?

b) Match the words with the right numbers.

cafeteria
classroom
playground
pupils
school
uniform

Who?

What?

I can see...

Where?

Wordgym → Go to your WB p. 11

2 **Listen to John.**
Who are his two friends?
Introduce them.

You: He... She...

→ Go to your WB p. 11

3 **Listen to the voices.**

a) Who is speaking?

b) Now play the silence game and say what you can hear outside the classroom.

You: I can hear...

→ Go to your WB p. 11

Listen and speak

CD ÉLÈVE PISTE 2

4 **a) Look at the first picture: who can you see? Imagine their name and age.**

b) → Go to your WB p. 12

Tactics

Écoute et concentre-toi sur les voix. Elles t'aideront à repérer qui parle : est-ce une voix féminine ou masculine ? Est-ce un adulte ou un enfant ?

Words to remember

CD CLASSE

- a class
- **ha**ppy
- a head**mas**ter
- new
- a **pu**pil
- a **tea**cher
- I think…
- Why?… Be**cause**…
- year 7

Don't forget!

1. BE

I'm happy.

Are you Australian?

He's from Scotland.

2. Les mots accentués

I think she's Australian.

You're happy to be back at school.

→ Go to your WB p. 13

QUICK CHECK → WB p. 16

Use what you know

5 Speak in pairs

Look at the school bulletin board. Ask and answer questions.

Pupil A: Who is... Where is...
Pupil B: He/She...

History	Mrs Preston • class 10
Maths	Mr Brain • class 14
English	Ms Monroe • class12
PE	Mr Grant • Gym
Biology	Mrs Toad • class 8
Art	Mrs Honey • class 3

6 Write a few lines

You have received an e-mail from your English pen friend. Write an answer.

From: nigel_kennedy@yahoo.com.uk
Object: back to school

Hi! How are you?
I'm so happy to go back to school because my friend Zach is in my class.
He's 12. My teachers are nice. My maths teacher is very cool.
My favourite teacher is Mrs Butterfly. She's very funny and I love history.
What about you? Are you happy to go back to school?
Nigel

HAVE FUN **Listen and sing along *Happy to go back to school.*** CD CLASSE

Go to your WB p. 14

YOUR TASK

7 Make a quiz about your school.

1. Prepare 3 questions about your teachers (name, subject and classroom).
2. Prepare 2 questions about the staff (headmaster, secretary).
3. Ask your classmates questions.

Go to your WB p. 14

Video Flash DVD

Come and visit my school!

Grammar

Be

Tu utilises **be** (« être ») pour présenter, situer ou décrire quelqu'un ou quelque chose.

I am a girl. *He is a boy.*

Forme affirmative	Forme interrogative	Forme négative
*I **am***	***Am** I?*	*I **am not***
*you **are***	***Are** you?*	*you **are not***
*he / she / it **is***	***Is** he / she / it?*	*he / she / it **is not***
*we / you / they **are***	***Are** we / you / they*	*we / you / they **are not***

→ À l'oral, les formes de **be** se contractent. La première lettre est remplacée par une apostrophe. Elle ne se prononce pas.

*I **am** → I'**m***
*you **are** → you'**re***
*he / she / it **is** → he'**s** / she'**s** / it'**s***

⚠ Pour dire l'âge, tu utilises **be**.

*Chad **is** eleven.*

Les questions

Dans les questions, le sujet est toujours **inversé**.

*Are **you** happy to be back at school?*
*Where is **she** from?*

→ Mémorise les **mots interrogatifs** :

Who?	Qui ?
Where?	Où ?
What?	Quoi ?
Why?	Pourquoi ?

Exercises

1 Complète les phrases suivantes avec le pronom personnel sujet qui convient.

a. My English teacher is Mrs Monroe.
... is very strict.
b. Tom and Chad are good friends.
... are happy to be in the same class.
c. How old are ... ?
d. ... am twelve.
e. Jane and I are sisters. ... are Australian.

2 Complète les phrases suivantes avec le verbe *be* à la forme affirmative, négative ou interrogative.

a. ... you Australian?
No, I ... . I ... American.
b. ... she from Boston?
No, she ... . She ... from New York.
c. Where ... you from? ... from Dublin.
d. Where ... they from?
They ... from Texas.
e. ... you late?
No we ... . It ... ten to eight.

3 Associe la question à la réponse.

a. Where are you from?
b. What's that?
c. Who's that boy?
d. Why are you smiling?
e. Is she Irish?

1. My brother, Jacob.
2. No, she isn't.
3. Chicago.
4. My pencil-case.
5. Because I'm happy.

More exercises → p. 154
CD élève Audio-Rom

ENGLISH LAB
CD classe

Les mots accentués

1 Écoute les phrases suivantes :

He's happy to be back at school.
He's happy because they're in the same class.

Dans une phrase anglaise, certains mots sont accentués, on les entend clairement : ils portent l'information principale.

2 Maintenant, lis ces phrases. N'oublie pas d'accentuer les mots importants. Écoute et vérifie tes réponses.

a. She's Australian and she's beautiful.
b. Mrs Monroe is a teacher. She's in classroom twelve.
c. He's excited because he's with his friend, Chad.

More exercises →
CD élève Audio-Rom

Language practice

Practise your vocabulary

1 Retrouve 7 mots se rapportant à l'école dans la grille ci-dessous. Écris-les dans ton cahier. Tu peux t'aider des dessins.

R	E	H	C	A	E	T	P
S	P	J	L	I	P	U	P
H	I	D	A	K	K	Y	H
T	R	N	S	I	H	G	E
A	K	U	S	E	I	O	N
M	Q	O	R	L	S	L	E
N	Y	R	O	P	T	O	P
Q	L	G	O	S	O	I	O
D	K	Y	M	W	R	B	K
Y	C	A	Z	V	Y	T	M
C	B	L	O	A	R	A	G
N	S	P	C	A	L	O	Q

2 Utilise ces dominos pour créer des mots.

class — gra — lo
tea — geo — bio
phy — gy — cher
room

3 Associe le mot interrogatif à sa réponse.

a. Where?
b. What?
c. Why?
d. Who?

1. Peter…
2. Because I…
3. In classroom 12.
4. It's a text book.

Practise your grammar

4 Complète les phrases suivantes avec le verbe *be* conjugué.

a. I … your new teacher.
b. How old … you? We … eleven, Sir.
c. Anna … Italian but she … in Italy at the moment.
d. Where … Peter and Jacob? They … in the cafeteria. Look! They … in the playground.
e. What's that? It … a sweet, Miss! It … my eraser.

5 Complète ces phrases avec *I* / *my* ; *you* / *your* ; *he* / *his* ; *she* / *her*.

a. Look at Lucy. … is with … friend.
b. Ben, have … got … book?
c. … name's David and … am French.
d. … isn't happy because … friend is absent.

Practise your pronunciation

CD CLASSE

6 a. Observe la phrase dite par cette élève anglaise. Quels sont les quatre mots les plus importants ?

b. Maintenant, entraîne-toi à bien prononcer cette phrase. Écoute pour vérifier ta prononciation.

Unit 2 I love history

Je vais m'entraîner à

- Comprendre des ordres et des demandes.
- Comprendre les consignes.
- Donner des ordres et demander quelque chose poliment.
- Faire un quiz sur l'histoire et la géographie.
- Préparer des questions pour un quiz.

Je vais utiliser

Can (1).............. p. 27

L'impératif.......... p. 27

Le lexique de l'école (2).

→ Go to your WB p. 10

Discover

1 Look at the drawing and imagine the teacher's instructions.

listen
sing
sleep
talk
write

Wordgym Go to your WB p. 17

2 Listen and match the drawings with the questions.

1 2 3 4

a) I don't understand. Can you explain?

b) I can't see. Can you move to one side, please?

c) I can't hear you. Can you repeat, please?

d) Miss, can I put my paper in the bin?

Go to your WB p. 17

3 Listen and speak about the people's emotions.

You: I think he/she's...

Listen and speak

CD ÉLÈVE PISTE 3

4 a) **Look at the first picture and guess what the subject of the class is.**

You: I think... because...

b) → Go to your WB p. 18

Tactics

Après avoir repéré qui parle, concentre-toi sur le ton des personnages. Tu pourras ainsi deviner s'ils sont en colère, tristes, surpris…

Words to remember

CD CLASSE

- **dif**ficult ≠ easy
- for**get**
- **his**tory
- in**cre**dible
- king
- queen
- talk

Don't forget!

1. CAN (1)

Can you open the window?

Can you repeat?

Can I come in?

2. L'accent de mot

difficult – incredible – repeat

→ Go to your WB p. 19

QUICK CHECK → WB p. 22

Use what you know

5 Speak in pairs

a) **Listen to the TV game.**

b) **Prepare questions about history and geography and quiz the class.**

You: Who is...? Where is...? Can you give the name of...?

→ Go to your WB p. 20

YOUR TASK

6 Be the club teacher.

Your teacher asks you to start the club.

1. Choose your club (football, dance, drama, art...).
2. Welcome the club members.
3. Give the club members 5 instructions. Be very polite!

B2i You can record yourself.

→ Go to your WB p. 20

Video Flash DVD

My favourite school club

Grammar

Can (1)

→ Tu utilises l'auxiliaire modal ***can*** pour **demander à quelqu'un de faire quelque chose.**
Can est toujours accompagné d'une base verbale (= un verbe non conjugué).
Can you close the door?

⚠ À la forme interrogative, le sujet se place entre ***can*** et la base verbale.
Can I come in?

L'impératif

→ Tu utilises l'impératif pour **donner des ordres** ou des **directives.**
Tu n'utilises pas de pronoms sujets mais simplement la **base verbale.**
Sit down!

⚠ N'oublie pas le point d'exclamation.

→ À la forme négative, tu ajoutes ***don't*** devant la base verbale.
Don't sit down!

→ À la première personne du pluriel, l'impératif permet de faire des **suggestions.** Il se construit avec ***let's*** suivi de la base verbale.
Let's talk about kings!

Exercises

1 Transforme les phrases suivantes pour demander s'il est possible de faire quelque chose.

a. Open the door.
b. Give me your book.
c. Come here.
d. Read the poem.
e. Answer my question.

2 Complète les phrases suivantes avec l'un des verbes à l'impératif.
close / don't give / let's read / sit down / hurry up / don't forget

a. We're late. …
b. … the door and …, please.
c. Are you ready? So, … the text now.
d. Peter! … your book next time!
e. Wait! … the answer now.

3 À partir de l'indice donné, fais des suggestions.

a. cinema → *Let's…*
b. a book → …
c. music → …
d. e-mail → …
e. song "Happy to come back to school" → …

⚠

More exercises → p. 154

CD ÉLÈVE Audio-Rom

ENGLISH LAB — L'accent de mot

CD CLASSE

1 En anglais, les mots comportant au moins deux syllabes sont accentués.
happy – repeat – Elizabeth – incredible

2 Écoute et répète les mots. Concentre-toi sur la syllabe accentuée.
moustache - exercise - magazine -silence - excellent - surprise

3 Écoute ce poème. Entraîne-toi à le répéter. Fais attention à l'accent de mot.

Summer is over
End of the holidays
Pupils go back to school
Teachers aren't very cool
Exercises and homework every day
Mathematics and Science
Biology and Technology
English and Spanish
Remember your lessons

More exercises →

CD ÉLÈVE Audio-Rom

Language practice

Practise your **vocabulary**

1 a. Remets les lettres dans l'ordre et copie les mots que tu as trouvés dans ton cahier.

G N I K — U Q N E E — K S A

L A T K — I W R E T — N L S I T E

b. Associe ces mots aux illustrations.

1 

2 

3 

4 

5 

6 

2 Trouve les lettres manquantes.

_ M B _ R R _ S S _ D

_ N G R _

S _ R P R _ S _ D

S _ D

_ X C _ T _ D

H _ P P _

3 Retrouve sept mots dans le serpent et copie-les dans ton cahier.

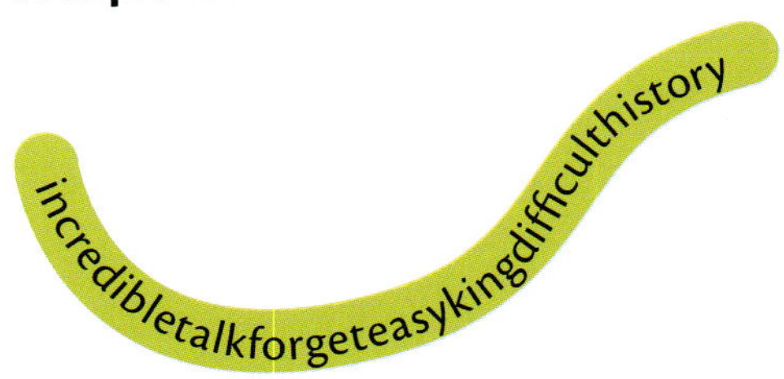

Practise your **grammar**

4 Transforme ces phrases en demandes polies.

a. Open the door!
b. I want a chocolate.
c. Give me a blue pen!
d. Clean the board!
e. I want to close the window.

5 Remets chaque phrase dans l'ordre.

a. you /please/ repeat / can / !
b. I / can / please/ go / board / the /to /?
c. name / give / you/ can / me / name/ queen / the / the / England / of /?

6 Que dis-tu à ton professeur d'anglais quand tu...

a. ... veux qu'il répète ?
b. ... veux aller aux toilettes ?
c. ... aimerais aider un camarade ?
d. ... veux écrire la réponse au tableau ?
e. ... veux sortir ?

Practise your **pronunciation**

CD CLASSE

7 Écoute et répète cette phrase plusieurs fois.

History, English and Maths are my favourite subjects.

Part 1 Check your progress

1 Listen

Stop chatting!

ton objectif Comprendre les règles de vie de classe.
L'impératif – *can*.

Écoute la conversation. Es-tu capable de :

- **A1** 1. dire qui parle et où se passe la scène ?
- 2. dire ce que cette personne demande ?
- **A1+** 3. repérer ses sentiments à la fin de la conversation ?

→ Go to your WB p. 24

2 Read

Can you help me?

ton objectif Comprendre un e-mail.
Can.

From: peter.bentley@yahoo.uk
to: cedric-dupont@orange.fr
Object: homework

Hi!
I have some French homework to do. Can you help me? Can you give me the name of your Prime Minister? Can you tell me where the President lives? Can you give me a quick reply?
Thanks!
Peter

Lis cet e-mail. Es-tu capable de :

- **A1** 1. dire ce qu'il / elle demande ?
- **A1+** 2. repérer qui a envoyé l'e-mail ? Dire sa nationalité ?
- 3. repérer qui est le destinataire ? Dire sa nationalité ?

→ Go to your WB p. 24

3 Speak

Pupils at Hogwarts

ton objectif Présenter un(e) élève.
Be au présent - Les pronoms personnels sujet - Les adjectifs possessifs.

Présente ces deux personnages.
Donne un maximum d'informations.

Name: Daniel Radcliffe (Harry Potter)
Date of birth: July 23, 1989
Nationality: British
Home town: Fulham, England

Name: Emma Watson (Hermione Granger)
Date of birth: April 15, 1990
Nationality: British
Home town: Oxford, England

Es-tu capable de :

- **A1** 1. donner des informations sur leur identité : nom, âge, nationalité, pays d'origine ?
- **A1+** 2. expliquer pourquoi tu les apprécies ?

→ Go to your WB p. 25

4 Write

English class rules

ton objectif Rédiger quelques règles de vie en classe.
L'impératif.
Nombre de mots 20

Écris quelques règles de vie en classe d'anglais.
Es-tu capable de :

- **A1** 1. noter 3 choses que tu dois faire ?
- 2. noter 3 choses que tu ne dois pas faire ?
- **A1+** 3. en faire une affiche (titre, couleurs, illustrations, mise en page) ?

→ Go to your WB p. 25

Part 1

Discovery

Year 7

Welcome to Teddington School. I'm Jacob. I'm 11 and I'm in year 7. My school is a secondary school in Richmond.

Did you know?

In a secondary school:
year 7 = 6ème
year 8 = 5ème
year 9 = 4ème
year 10 = 3ème

Uniforms

The pupils in my school wear uniforms. I like it. I think the girls in my school are very pretty.

Timetable

This is my timetable. It's quite cool because I finish at 3 o'clock every day and I haven't got lessons on Saturdays.

My favourite subject is Maths. What about you?

Time	Monday	Tuesday	Wednesday	Thursday	Friday
8.30 – 8.50 am	Assembly	Form time	Form time	Assembly	Form time
8.50 – 9.50 am	Design and technology	PSHE	Religious education	Music	PE
9.50 – 10.50 am	Science	English	Science	English	French
10.50 – 11.10 am	Break	Break	Break	Break	Break
11.10 – 12.10	English	Art	ICT	History	English
12.10 – 12.55	Lunch	Lunch	Lunch	Lunch	Lunch
1 – 2 pm	Maths	PE	Geography	Maths	Science
2 – 3 pm	History	French	Maths	Science	Geography
	Clubs	Clubs	Clubs	Clubs	Clubs

Did you know?

ICT: Information and Communication Technologies
PE: Physical education
PSHE: Personal, Social and Health Education
Form time= vie de classe

Assembly

We have assembly on Mondays and Thursdays at 8.30. All year 7 pupils meet in the hall. We listen to the headmaster. He gives us important information about the school.

Lunch box

Lunch-time

I don't eat at the school cafeteria when it's sunny. I take my lunch box!

Quiz time

Read and answer the questions.

1. How old is a pupil in year 7?
2. What is the school uniform?
3. What is ICT?
4. When and where do pupils have assembly?

FINAL TASK

1. **Play the "10 questions game".**
   Read the game instructions.

Game instructions

- Ask your classmates 10 questions.
- Ask the player to choose the type of question:
  - *Yes/no* questions count for 1 point.
  - *Wh-* questions count for 3 points.
- The winner is the player with the highest score.

2. Create your set of questions.
   a) Imagine different topics: school in the UK, history, geography, PE, etc.
   b) Ask different types of questions.
3. Play the game with your schoolmates.
4. Say who the winner is.

www.teddington.richmond.sch.uk

Part 2 Home, sweet home

A mouse in my house

CD ÉLÈVE PISTE 4 Karaoké

A new friend, a new buddy,
I've got a little mouse in my study.
He's got a red hat,
He loves my old cat,
And in the kitchen, he plays with the kitten.
He likes cake, he likes jelly.
He likes candy bars dipped in honey!
But he doesn't like cheese! 'Coz it makes him sneeze!
He doesn't like bread! It makes his nose red!

Chorus
Oh yes I'm happy! I know I'm lucky!
I've got a little mouse in my house! (...)

Unit 3

Come in!

Je vais m'entraîner à

- Comprendre des informations sur une maison.
- Comprendre une description dans une carte postale.
- Présenter la maison de quelqu'un.
  Décrire une pièce de la maison.
- Me renseigner sur ce que quelqu'un possède.
- Imaginer la chambre d'une célébrité.

Je vais utiliser

Have got .... p. 37

Le lexique de la maison.

→ Go to your WB p. 26

Discover

1 Listen, look at the house and react.

a) Listen and repeat.

b) Listen and match the words with the right numbers.

bathroom
bed
bedroom
chair
desk
kitchen
lamp
living-room
shelves
window

c) Now describe the house: What can you see?

You: The bed is…

You: I can see a… He's in… / It's on…

on
in
under
next to

Wordgym → Go to your WB p. 27

2 Listen and find information about Mr Butler.

You: He's got…

3 Listen and say where the people are.

You: They are in… because I can hear…

→ Go to your WB p. 27

Listen and speak

CD ÉLÈVE PISTE 5

4 **Look at the first picture: where are the boys? Now listen and find information about them.**

→ Go to your WB p. 28

Tactics

À la première écoute, concentre-toi sur les bruits que tu entends. Ils te permettront d'en déduire où les personnes se trouvent.

Words to remember

CD CLASSE

- a **bed**room
- a com**pu**ter
- a desk
- a door
- a home
- a house
- pets
- **up**stairs/**down**stairs

Don't forget!

1. HAVE GOT

- *Have you got a TV in your room?*
- *I've got hamsters.*
- *Zoe's got a cat.*

2. La lettre « a » (1)

- *cat* /kaet/
- *game* /geɪm/

→ Go to your WB p. 29

QUICK CHECK → WB p. 32

Use what you know

5 Speak in pairs

a) Ask and answer questions about the things in your bedroom. Speak about furniture (desk, bed...), electronics (PCs, TV...), toys...

Pupil A: Have you got...? How many...? Where...?
Pupil B: Yes... No...

b) Then report to the class.

Pupil A: He/she's got...

Go to your WB p. 30

6 Speak for a minute

Look at the postcard. Read it and say who lives in this room. Justify your answer. Use words you know.

You: I think it's... because... but...

Hi!
I'm in Chicago with my parents and we are in a great museum. Have a look at this bedroom and guess who lives there! He's got glasses but he hasn't got a hat. He's got a broom. His best friends are Ron and Hermione.
See you

Steve Smith

YOUR TASK

7 Write a short note for the school magazine about your favourite star's bedroom.

1. Choose a star and imagine his or her bedroom.
2. List what he/she's got in his/her room.
3. Give details (colours, numbers, location).
4. Organize your ideas and write a paragraph.

Go to your WB p. 30

Video Flash DVD

Come and visit my house!

Grammar

■ Have got

→ Tu utilises **have got** quand tu veux dire que tu possèdes quelque chose.

Forme affirmative	Forme interrogative	Forme négative
You**'ve got** a computer.	**Have** you **got** a computer?	You **haven't got** a computer.
He/She**'s got** a computer.	**Has** he/she **got** a computer?	He/She **hasn't got** a computer.

→ À l'oral, à la forme affirmative, on emploie la forme contractée.

*I**'ve got** a TV in my room.*

→ **Have** devient **has** (ou **'s** à la forme contractée) à la troisième personne du singulier.

*He**'s got** a lot of DVDs.*

⚠ Ne confonds pas la forme contractée **'s** (= has) et **'s** (= is).

*He**'s got** a computer. (= He has)*
*He**'s** American. (= He is)*

⚠ À la forme interrogative, il faut inverser le sujet et l'auxiliaire **have**.

***Have** you **got** a little sister?*

→ On emploie la forme pleine **have** dans les questions, les négations et les réponses brèves (*short answers*).

***Have** you **got** a computer?*
*Yes, I **have**. / No, I **haven't**.*

⚠ Dans les réponses brèves, **got** disparaît.

Exercises

1 Dis si tu possèdes les objets suivants. Rédige des phrases complètes.

a. a computer?
b. DVDs?
c. a television?
d. a CD player?
e. rock star posters?

2 *Have* ou *has* ? Complète ces questions et réponds.

a. ... you got a lot of friends?
b. ... Tom got a lot of DVDs?
c. ... you got a TV in your room?
d. ... Tom and Chad got pets?
e. ... Zoe got a big brother?

3 *Is* ou *has* ? Lis ces phrases et indique si *'s* correspond à *is* ou à *has*.

a. He's my brother.
b. She's got a computer in her room.
c. He's got new DVDs.
d. She's a nice little girl.
e. He's got an old desk.

More exercises → p. 154

CD élève Audio-Rom

English Lab — La lettre « a » (1)

CD classe

1 Écoute les mots suivants :

cat – table – that – game

2 Tu remarques que la lettre « a » peut se prononcer :

/ae/	/ei/
comme dans cat	comme dans Jake

3 Lis ces phrases à voix haute en tenant compte de la bonne prononciation des « a » :

a. *The cat is on the table.*
b. *Kate has got lots of games.*
c. *Jack has got a big black rat in his bag.*
d. *Jake hasn't got his pencil-case.*

More exercises → CD élève Audio-Rom

Language practice

Practise your vocabulary

1 Es-tu capable de nommer :

a. 2 objets commençant par la lettre "c" et se trouvant dans une chambre ?
b. 3 pièces de la maison se terminant par *room* ?
c. 2 pièces de la maison ne se terminant pas par *room* ?
d. 3 objets se trouvant dans le salon ?

2 Complète avec le mot qui convient :

a. I haven't got a TV in my... but I've got a computer. It's on my...
b. She has got a new fridge in her...
c. My dad is watching TV in the...
d. I live in a big... in the country.
e. We've got three...: a cat, a dog and a rabbit.

3 Trouve les lettres manquantes.

D □ □ K

S H □ □ F

U □ S T □ I □ S

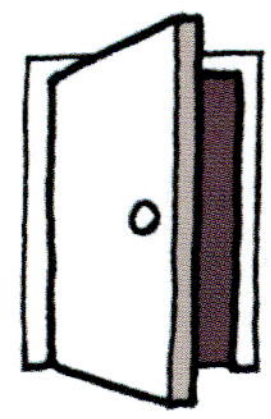
D □ □ R

Practise your grammar

4 Conjugue *have got* à la forme affirmative ou négative et à la personne qui convient.

a. She ... a big desk but she ... a computer.
b. I ... ... a TV in my room but I ... ... a CD player.
c. They... dogs because they are allergic to pets.
d. My sister... a shelf in her bedroom but she... lots of books.
e. Ben and Jake ... ... a great house.
f. We... a new cage for our hamster.

5 Retrouve deux phrases dans le serpent et réécris-les. Ajoute la ponctuation et les espaces, puis réponds à la question.

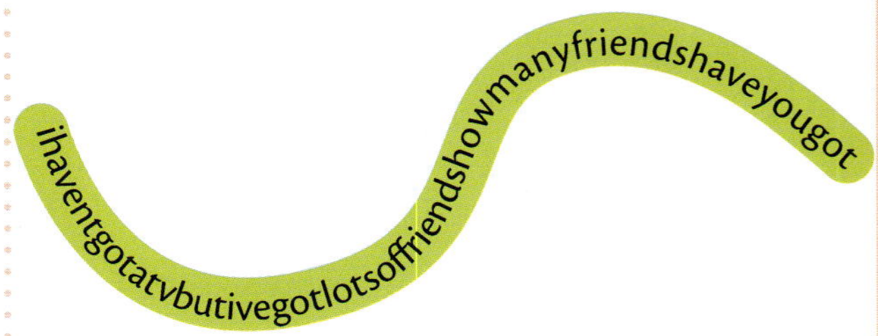

Practise your pronunciation

CD CLASSE

6 Lis les phrases suivantes à voix haute. Écoute et vérifie tes réponses.

a. Matt 's my best mate.
b. Jack and Jake have got a lot of games.
c. Jane 's got a rabbit. His name's Brad.
d. Sam 's late because he hasn't got his skates.

Unit 4 A garden party

Je vais m'entraîner à

- Comprendre ce qu'une personne aime ou n'aime pas.
- Comprendre un court poème sur les goûts de quelqu'un.
- Présenter un personnage et parler de ses goûts.
- Interroger mes camarades sur leur identité et sur leurs goûts.
- Écrire un poème sur mes goûts.

Je vais utiliser

Le présent simple... p. 43

Le lexique de la nourriture et des loisirs.

Go to your WB p. 26

Discover

1 Food: What words do you know?

a) Listen and spot the words you know.

b) Match the words and the pictures.

ice cream – cake – salad – sausages – vegetables – water – fruit – milk – chicken – orange juice – chips – baked beans

Wordgym → Go to your WB p. 33

2 Listen and say what the boy likes and doesn't like.

→ Go to your WB p. 33

You: The boy likes… He doesn't like…

3 Listen to the characters' reactions and say how they feel.

Use: sorry – excited – It hurts! – He/She likes it! – He/She doesn't like it!
You: The boy is…

Listen and speak

CD ÉLÈVE PISTE 6

4 **Look at the first picture and imagine their conversation.**
Now, listen and speak about the party.

Go to your WB p. 34

Tactics

Écoute et repère les onomatopées (*Wow! Oops! Ouch! Shh! Pooh! Yuck! Yummy!*) qu'utilisent les personnages pour en déduire leurs sentiments et mieux comprendre l'histoire.

Words to remember

CD CLASSE

- drink
- eat
- live
- play
- work
- food
- the **gar**den
- **hun**gry
- a **par**ty
- **thir**sty

Don't forget!

1. Le présent simple

I like...
I don't like...
He lives...
He doesn't live...

2. La lettre « a » (2)

late /leɪt/ *party* /pɑːtɪ/
dad /daed/ *care* /kɛər/

Go to your WB p. 35

QUICK CHECK → WB p. 38

Use what you know

5 Speak for a minute

You're part of the TV show "Pop Idol". Introduce yourself to the audience: identity, family, likes and dislikes, hobbies.

You: Hi! I'm... I live... I have got... My dad/mum works in... I like... I don't like...

6 Speak in pairs

Interview a classmate (identity, likes and dislikes, hobbies) and recap the information to the class.

Pupil A: What's...? Do you like...?
Pupil B: My name... I...

→ Go to your WB p. 36

YOUR TASK

7 Write a poem and illustrate it.

1. Read the poem and then listen to it.
2. Now say if you like chips, burgers and beans.
3. Create a poem with the food you like and don't like. Illustrate it.

CD CLASSE

Chips are nice,
Chips are yummy,
I like chips in my tummy!

Burgers are nice,
Burgers are yummy,
I like burgers in my tummy!

Baked beans are nice,
Baked beans are yummy,
I like baked beans in my tummy!

By Nicola Singyard

Video Flash DVD

Dinner at home

Grammar

■ Le présent simple (1)

→ Tu utilises le **présent simple** pour parler des **caractéristiques de quelqu'un** (ce qu'il aime, où il habite, ce qu'il fait dans la vie...).

*He **lives** and **works** in New York.* *I **love** barbecue.*
*You **eat** too much!*

→ À la forme affirmative, le verbe ne se conjugue pas : on utilise la base verbale.

*I **like**... I **work**... You **eat**...*

⚠ À la troisième personne du singulier (**she** / **he** / **it**), il faut ajouter un **-s** à la base verbale.

*He live**s** and work**s** in New York.*

Remarque : Après **go**, ou les verbes se terminant par **-ch** et **-sh**, on ajoute **-es**.

*He go**es**... He watch**es**...*

→ À la forme interrogative, on emploie **do** (**does** à la troisième personne du singulier).

***Do** you like your life in England?* *Where **does** he live?*

→ À la forme négative, on utilise ***do*** / ***does*** suivi de ***not***.

*I **do not** live in New York.* *He **does not** live in England.*

Remarque : On utilise souvent une forme contractée.
do + not = **don't**
does + not = **doesn't**

⚠ À la forme interrogative et à la forme négative, on utilise toujours la base verbale, même à la troisième personne du singulier. C'est **does / doesn't** qui porte la marque « s ».

Does he like barbecue? *He doesn't like chips.*

Exercises

1 Conjugue les verbes suivants au présent simple.

a. We (*love*) tomato salad.
b. Scarlett's father (*live*) in New York.
c. His parents (*work*) in Oxford.
d. She (*go*) to school in London.
e. Chad (*want*) to drink Coke.

2 Complète ces questions avec *do* ou *does* et réponds-y.

a. ... Tom and Chad know Scarlett's father?
b. ... Chad like sausages?
c. What ... Chad want to drink?
d. Where ... Scarlett's father live?
e. ... you like barbecue food?

3 Complète ces phrases à la forme négative du présent simple.

a. He ... live in England.
b. No, I ... want to drink Coke. I ... like it!
c. They ... work in England.
d. Scarlett's mother ... think it is a good idea.
e. We ... work in a hotel, we work in a restaurant.

More exercises → p. 154

CD ÉLÈVE Audio-Rom

ENGLISH LAB — La lettre « a » (2)

CD CLASSE

1 Tu as appris à reconnaître les sons /ae/ comme dans « **dad** », et /ei/ comme dans « **Jake** ».
La voyelle **« a »** peut également se prononcer /aː/ comme dans « **star** » ou /ə/ comme dans « **care** ».

cat → Kate car → scared
/ae/ /eɪ/ /aː/ /ea/

2 Écoute ce poème. Entraîne-toi à le répéter. Fais attention à la prononciation des lettres « a ».

Kate's cat is a star.
He's as brave as dogs are
And he's got a black hat.
His best pal is a rat,
Never pale, never scared!

Oh yes, he doesn't care
And at night, in his car
Yes, he stares at the stars
And he plays the guitar.
Yes, Kate's cat is a star!

More exercises → CD ÉLÈVE Audio-Rom

Language practice

Practise your vocabulary

1 Écoute et répète ce poème en imitant le bruit du train. Utilise les mots que tu connais pour inventer une suite.

Cheese and biscuits, cheese and biscuits
Beef and carrots, beef and carrots
Soup, soup!
Eggs and chicken, eggs and chicken
Beans and pork chops, beans and pork chops
Soup, soup!

2 Classe les mots suivants dans les catégories d'aliments indiquées.

chicken – potatoes – pork – beef – milk – cake – chocolate – salad – water – beans – Coke – sausages – ice cream – carrots

1. Meat 2. Vegetables 3. Drinks 4. Sweets

3 Associe les mots suivants à leur définition. Trouve l'intrus.

football – a photographer – milk – a carrot – ice-cream

a. This person takes photos.
b. It's a delicious dessert.
c. It's an orange vegetable.
d. It's a drink.

HAVE FUN **Say this tongue-twister.**
Chris eats crisps, chips and chicken at Christmas!

Practise your grammar

4 Complète les phrases suivantes avec le verbe qui convient : *live, like, speak, eat, drink, play*. N'oublie pas de le conjuguer.

a. She... crisps but she... chips.
b. A lot of English people... bacon and... tea.
c. I... tennis but I... basket ball.
d. Ben and Jake ... in a great house.
e. We... French and English.

5 Réponds à ces questions selon le modèle et ajoute une information supplémentaire si nécessaire.

→ *Do you like spinach? No, I don't but I like beans.*

a. Do you like soup?
b. Do you like hamburgers?
c. Do you play cricket?
d. Do you watch TV every day?
e. Do you eat sausages for breakfast?

Practise your pronunciation

6 Regarde bien l'orthographe des mots suivants et déduis-en la prononciation du « a ». Classe-les dans un tableau.

Jake – Jack – Matt – bare – mate – dad – stare – pack – car – cake – black – bar – back – snake – snack – care – bake – star

/ae/	/ei/	/aː/	/ea/
...	...	...	...

7 Écoute cette chanson et chante-la.

In my house, I've got many nice rooms,
Bathrooms, a kitchen and a large living-room...

Part 2 Check your progress

1 Listen

My house

ton objectif Comprendre un adolescent qui décrit sa chambre et ses habitudes.

Be • *Have got* • Les prépositions de lieu.

Écoute cet adolescent te parler de lui et de sa chambre. Es-tu capable de :

A1
1. relever des informations concernant son identité, et ses goûts ?

A1+
2. comprendre la description de sa maison et de sa chambre ?
3. comprendre la réaction de ses parents ?

→ Go to your WB p. 40

2 Read

My grandma

ton objectif Comprendre la rédaction d'une petite fille sur le mode de vie d'une personne de sa famille.

Be • Le présent simple • *Have got* • Les prépositions de lieu.

I love my grandma! Her name is Heather and she is 71 years old. She lives in a comfortable house in a small town next to London. She's got a big kitchen in her house, and she cooks very well! She's got four cats. They are nice. She's got lots of books too. She reads a lot! Grandma loves sports! She's got a piano. She plays every day. I think she's very good! I really love my grandma! She's a star for me!

Sarah Parker.

Lis le texte de Sarah. Es-tu capable de :

A1
1. repérer de qui elle parle dans son texte ?
2. décrire la maison de cette personne ?

A1+
3. décrire ses goûts et ses activités ?
4. expliquer la dernière phrase ?

→ Go to your WB p. 40

3 Speak

My favourite pet

ton objectif Décrire son animal familier préféré.

Like • Le présent simple • Les prépositions de lieu.

30 secondes

Présente ton animal familier préféré à la classe. Es-tu capable de :

A1
1. présenter l'animal (identité, lieu de vie, goûts) ?

A1+
2. dire quels sont ses endroits préférés dans la maison, dans ta chambre, quand tu joues avec lui ?

→ Go to your WB p. 41

4 Write

My new friend!

ton objectif Rédiger un paragraphe au sujet d'un(e) ami(e).

Be • La présentation • Le présent simple • *Have got.*

Nombre de mots 40

Écris un paragraphe sur un(e) nouvel(le) ami(e). Présente-le (la), décris sa chambre, parle de sa maison et de ce qu'il / elle aime faire dans la vie. Es-tu capable de :

A1
1. présenter ton ami (identité) ?

A1+
2. parler de sa famille (parents, frères et sœurs) ?
3. décrire sa maison, sa chambre ?
4. parler de ses goûts ?

→ Go to your WB p. 41

Part 2

Discovery

The British lifestyle

Hi there!
I'm Julia, I'm English and I live in Kingston.
Here are some photos of my house.

Traditional homes in the United Kingdom

Look at the green house with the bay window. This is my home.

My best friend Emily is very lucky because she lives in a beautiful cottage in the country.

Home, sweet home

This is our living-room. It's my mum's favourite room. It's so cosy! Can you guess when we took the photo?

English breakfast

Breakfast with Grandma! She loves eggs with bacon and toast. She also likes baked beans! Yuk! Yuk!

Afternoon tea

Five p.m.:
tea time with my friends. We had biscuits and cakes too.

Did you know?

The British love tea. It's their favourite drink! They drink 5 or 6 cups of tea a day!

Quiz time

Can you...

1. say where Julia lives?
2. name a typical form of window?
3. name 3 things in Julia's living-room?
4. say what her grandmother eats for breakfast?
5. explain what tea time is?

FINAL TASK

You are a script writer: create a hero for a TV series and describe his/her lifestyle.

1. Give information about your hero: name, age, city, family, pets...
2. Describe his/her home: city or country, type of house, rooms, furniture, objects...
3. Imagine what he/she likes (food, pets, hobbies...).
4. Be original. Your hero can be funny or strange.

http://www.woodlands-junior.Kent.sch.uk/customs/questions/house.html

Part 3 Let's take a tour

Ghosts

CD ÉLÈVE PISTE 7 Karaoké

There's a ghost in the castle, there's a ghost
In the night, in the dark, yes he goes
To the top of the tower
Where he shows his scary power
There's a ghost, there's a ghost!

There's a ghost in the tower, there's a ghost
Look up there! He can move like shadows
He can fly, he can slide
He's unnoticed in the night
There's a ghost, there's a ghost

Chorus

So you must decide if you want to risk the night
Are you brave? Are you scared?
Are you very well prepared?
Take your sword, and your armour: it's tonight...
Are you ready for the fight! For the fight! For the fight?...

Part 3

Unit 5 Welcome to the Tower of London!

Je vais m'entraîner à

- Comprendre où se situent précisément des choses.
- Comprendre les informations essentielles d'une brochure touristique.
- Décrire un lieu, dire ce que l'on y trouve.
- Me renseigner sur ce que l'on trouve dans un lieu particulier. Acheter des souvenirs.
- Raconter brièvement une visite touristique.

Je vais utiliser

There is/There are .... p. 53

How much/How many ... p. 53

Le lexique lié à la visite de monuments.

→ Go to your WB p. 42

Discover

1 Listen to the poem and say it.

Spiders, spiders everywhere!
On the table, under the chair!
In my schoolbag, next to the bed
Behind the door and on my head!
Spiders, spiders everywhere!
But I'm not scared
And I don't care!

→ Go to your WB p. 43

2 Listen, look at the drawing and react.

a) Listen and repeat.

b) Speak about the ghosts.
How many are there? Where are they?
You: There's a ghost… There are two ghosts…
Use: in, on, under, next to, behind, in front of, between

1 painting
2 fireplace
3 raven
4 clock
5 crown
6 sword

Wordgym → Go to your WB p. 43

3 Read this list of words.

a) Translate them into French. Say why they are easy to understand.

a table | a monster | a poem | historic | a collection | a visit | torture | dangerous

b) Listen to the words and repeat. React.

Read and speak

4 **Look at the document. Read it carefully and say why it's an interesting visit.**

You: I would like to visit it because...

→ Go to your WB p. 44

Tactics

Certains mots anglais sont faciles à comprendre à l'écrit car ils ressemblent beaucoup au français. Ce sont les mots « transparents ». Ils t'aideront à comprendre le sens d'un document écrit.

Welcome to the Tower of London

Opening times

Tuesday – Saturday	09:00 am – 04:30 pm
Sunday – Monday	10:00 am – 04:30 pm

Prices Adult £17

Child (Under 16) £9.50

The White Tower
It is one of the most famous castles in the United Kingdom.

The Ravens
There are seven ravens at the Tower today. They are usually near Wakefield Tower. The ravens eat 170g of meat a day, plus bird biscuits soaked in blood.

The Crown Jewels
Come and see the Queen's jewels: a collection of 23,578 gems including the beautiful Imperial State Crown.

The Beefeaters
They are the famous guards of the Tower of London. They organize very interesting visits of the Tower.

Ghosts, ghosts everywhere!
Many people were tortured and executed at the Tower. Watch out for their ghosts!

Don't forget to visit the gift shop for souvenirs!
Visit us at **http://www.hrp.org.uk/TowerOfLondon/**

Fascinating London!
If you want to discover **historic London**, don't forget to visit Westminster Abbey and Saint Paul's Cathedral! There are **great museums:** the British Museum **(www.britishmuseum.org)** and Madame Tussaud's, the famous wax works museum.

Words to remember

CD CLASSE

- a **castle**
- a **crown**
- **famous**
- a **ghost**
- I **want**/ I **don't want**
- a **jewel**
- a **king**
- the **price**
- a **queen**
- a **raven**
- a **tower**

Don't forget!

1. There is/There are

There is *a ghost at the window.*

There are *seven ravens at the Tower of London.*

2. La contraction de *there is/there are*

/ðɛaʳz/ /ðɛaʳ/

→ Go to your WB p. 45

QUICK CHECK → WB p. 48

Use what you know

5 Speak for a minute

Look at the pictures and spot the differences.

You: In picture A, there's a cat on the table but in picture B, there's a cat under the table.

A

B

6 Write a few lines

Write a postcard to your friend about your visit to the Tower of London.
Explain why the Tower of London is an interesting monument.

→ Go to your WB p. 46

YOUR TASK

7 Buy souvenirs in a shop.

CD CLASSE

1. Listen to the conversation and complete it in your workbook.
2. Define roles (the shopkeeper, the customer). Decide what you would like to buy.
3. Act out the conversation in the shop.

a. The shopkeeper says what there is in his shop.

b. The customer decides what he wants to buy.

→ Go to your WB p. 46

Video Flash DVD

Shopping

Grammar

■ There is / there are

On utilise **there is / there are** pour dire **ce qu'il y a quelque part**, pour **informer quelqu'un** de l'existence de quelque chose.

Singulier	Pluriel
There is + nom au singulier	***There are*** + nom au pluriel
There is a spider on the table.	***There are*** two ghosts in the castle.

⚠ Pour poser une question, n'oublie pas d'inverser **be** et le sujet :

__Is there__ a spider on the table?
__Are there__ ghosts in the castle?

⚠ On répond à ces questions par des réponses courtes :

Yes, there is/are. *No, there isn't/aren't.*

■ How much / how many

→ On utilise **how much** pour demander le **prix d'un article dans un magasin**.

__How much__ is the pencil? It's 99p.

→ On utilise **how many** pour demander **combien d'éléments il y a**.

__How many__ spiders are there under the table?
There are three spiders.

Exercises

1 Complète ces phrases avec *there is / there are* à la forme qui convient. Traduis-les ensuite en français.

a. … ravens at the Tower of London.
b. … many tourists at the Tower today.
c. … a ghost in the castle.
d. … big black spiders in your bedroom? No, …
e. … a black cat next to the clock.

2 Complète les questions suivantes avec *how much* ou *how many* à la forme qui convient. Traduis-les ensuite en français.

a. … is the t-shirt?
b. … mugs would you like?
c. … ghosts are there in the Tower of London?
d. … are the mugs?
e. … money have you got?

3 Retrouve les questions qui ont provoqué ces réponses.

a. The key ring is £1.50.
b. There are seven ravens at the Tower of London.
c. I have got three white t-shirts.
d. The miniature Towers are £12.99.
e. The ravens are near Wakefield Tower.

More exercises → p. 154 CD ÉLÈVE Audio-Rom

ENGLISH LAB (CD CLASSE) La contraction de « there is », « there are »

There is / there are se prononcent presque toujours de manière contractée.
There is → ***There's***
There are ne se contracte pas à l'écrit, mais à l'oral, l'auxiliaire « *are* » disparaît presque totalement.

1 Écoute ces deux phrases et répète-les.

There's a spider on the wall.
There are two ravens at the door.

2 Écoute cette chanson et chante-la en prenant soin de bien prononcer « there's » et « there are ».

Dark dark house (x2)
There's a spider on the wall!
Crawl, crawl, crawl!
There are two ravens at the door!
Caw, caw, caw!
There's a mouse on the floor!
And there are two ghosts behind the door! (…)

More exercises → CD ÉLÈVE Audio-Rom

Language practice

Practise your vocabulary

1 Retrouve les mots correspondant aux définitions suivantes.

a. It's a black bird. There are seven of them at the Tower of London.
b. Kings and Queens have got one. They wear it on their heads.
c. It's a very large house with towers.
d. It's a shop where there are souvenirs.
e. It's a beautiful object.

2 Regarde la vitrine de ce magasin de souvenirs et dis ce que tu veux acheter.

Practise your grammar

3 Regarde le dessin et réponds aux questions.

a. How many chairs are there?
b. How many clocks are there?
c. How many paintings are there?
d. Where is the spider?
e. Where are the ghosts?
f. Where are the paintings?

4 Écoute les phrases et dis quelle forme tu entends : *they're* ou *there*.

Practise your pronunciation

5 Écoute le poème et répète-le. Attention à bien prononcer *there's*.

In the dark dark wood,
There's a dark dark castle
And in the dark dark castle,
There's a dark dark tower!
And in the dark dark tower,
There's a dark dark room
And in that dark dark room,
There's a dark dark box
And in the dark dark box,
There's a GHOST!

HAVE FUN

Say this tongue-twister!
There are three of their dogs over there!
They're happy, they're happy!
They're not scared!

Unit 6 A scary visit

Je vais m'entraîner à

Comprendre un itinéraire.

Comprendre des recommandations.
Comprendre les règles à respecter lors de la visite d'un monument.

Indiquer un itinéraire à quelqu'un.
Donner les règles à suivre lors de la visite d'un monument.

Me renseigner sur ce que quelqu'un est capable de faire.
Me renseigner sur un itinéraire.

Écrire le programme de la visite d'un château.

Je vais utiliser

Can (2) .... p. 59

Must................ p. 59

Want to .... p. 59

Le lexique lié à la peur, aux itinéraires.

Les parties du corps.

→ Go to your WB p. 42

Discover

1 Can you tell me the way?

a) Look at the signs, listen and repeat.

b) Listen and draw the itinerary.

→ Go to your WB p. 49

2

a) Look at the pictures. Then listen to the conversation.
Use the words you understand to put the pictures in chronological order.

b) Listen again. Say where they want to go. Then speak about Zoe's problems.

Wordgym → Go to your WB p. 49

A

B

C

Listen and speak

CD ÉLÈVE PISTE 8

3 **Listen to the conversation.**
Speak about the children's itinerary.
Then speak about their visit.

→ Go to your WB p. 50

Tactics

Regarde bien les illustrations : elles t'aideront à comprendre ce que tu entends.

Words to remember

CD CLASSE

- **beaut**iful
- **dan**gerous
- dark
- **fin**ger
- leg
- nose
- scared
- a **vi**sit
- a souve**nir**

Don't forget!

1. CAN (2)/MUST

They can run.
They can't fly.
We must hurry.
Visitors mustn't bring food.

2. La prononciation de *can / can't*

/kæn/
/kən/
/kaːnt/

→ Go to your WB p. 51

QUICK CHECK → WB p. 54

Use what you know

4 Speak for a minute

a) Look at the documents. Speak about the pupils' future visit to Dover Castle and about the teacher's recommendations.

- Be ready for the visit!
- History books about Henry VIII (p. 65–66)
- sandwiches (lunch picnic)
- £5 for souvenirs
- a raincoat or an umbrella
- no MP3 players, no electronic games!

b) Your best friend is absent. Write him an email about the teacher's recommendations for the trip.

→ Go to your WB p. 52

5 Speak in pairs

Challenge your friends and play the "Can you" game!

Pupil A: Can you touch your leg with your nose?
Pupil B: Yes, I can / No, I can't.

YOUR TASK

6 Tell me the way.

You're at the Tower of London and want to go to Buckingham Palace. You haven't got a map. You call your English friend who tells you the way.

1. Define roles.
2. Use the map of London p. 62 to make up the itinerary.
3. Act out the conversation.

→ Go to your WB p. 52

Video Flash DVD

The London Dungeon

Grammar

■ Can/can't (2)

➜ Tu utilises l'auxiliaire modal ***can / can't*** pour parler de ce **qu'une personne est capable de faire ou pas**.

*Ghosts **can** fly!*
*Zoe **can't** walk fast.*

➜ **Rappel** : L'auxiliaire ***can*** permet aussi de formuler une demande ou de demander une permission.

***Can** I open the window?*

■ Must/mustn't

➜ Tu utilises l'auxiliaire modal ***must / mustn't*** pour parler de ce qu'une personne doit faire **(obligation)** ou ne doit pas faire **(interdiction)**.

*You **must** turn right.*
*You **mustn't** use your mobile phones.*

■ Want (to)

➜ Tu utilises le verbe ***want*** pour dire ce que tu veux ou ne veux pas faire.

*I **want** two mugs please.*
*We **want to** buy souvenirs.*
*I **don't want to** go to the cinema.*

⚠ À la 3ème personne du singulier, tu ajoutes un **s** au verbe et tu utilises **doesn't** à la place de **don't** :

*He **wants** to visit the Tower of London.*
*He **doesn't want to** visit Buckingham Palace.*

Exercises

1 Dis ce que l'on doit faire lors de la visite d'un monument historique ou pas.

a. eat snacks
b. be quiet
c. listen to music on an MP3 player
d. listen to the guide
e. use a mobile phone

2 Complète les phrases suivantes avec *can, can't, must, mustn't*. Traduis les phrases en français.

a. The visit starts in 10 minutes. We ... go and buy the tickets now!
b. This is a very old monument! You ... be quiet and you ... run around!
c. Little girls ... run very fast because they have got little legs.
d. I ... speak German but I ... speak English very well.
e. To go to Buckingham Palace, you ... cross Saint James's park.

3 Dis ce que les personnages suivants veulent ou ne veulent pas faire pendant leur séjour à Londres. Puis dis ce que toi, tu veux faire ou pas pendant ton séjour.

a. **Patrick:** Tower of London / a good restaurant / ~~Hyde Park~~
b. **Kate:** Buckingham Palace / a musical / ~~Tower of London~~
c. **John and Brian:** Trafalgar Square / British Museum / ~~Westminster Abbey~~

More exercises ➜ p. 154

CD ÉLÈVE Audio-Rom

ENGLISH LAB — La prononciation de CAN/CAN'T

CD CLASSE

1 Écoute ces phrases.

Tom can run very fast. *Can ghosts run?*
No, they can't but they can fly.

Can se prononce de trois façons différentes :

/kən/	/kæn/	/kɑːnt/

2 Lis ces phrases à voix haute en tenant compte de la bonne prononciation de *can*.

a. Ghosts can fly but they can't run.
b. Zoe can't walk fast: she's got little legs.
c. Can we use a mobile phone at the Tower of London? No, we can't!
d. Can I have the ring? Of course you can!

More exercises ➜ CD ÉLÈVE Audio-Rom

Language practice

Practise your vocabulary

1 a) Écoute la chanson et trouve les mots qui correspondent aux chiffres qui figurent sur le dessin.

b) Chante la chanson.

Head, shoulders, knees and toes
Knees and toes
Head, shoulders, knees and toes
Knees and toes
Eyes and ears, and mouth and nose
Head, shoulders, knees and toes
Knees and toes

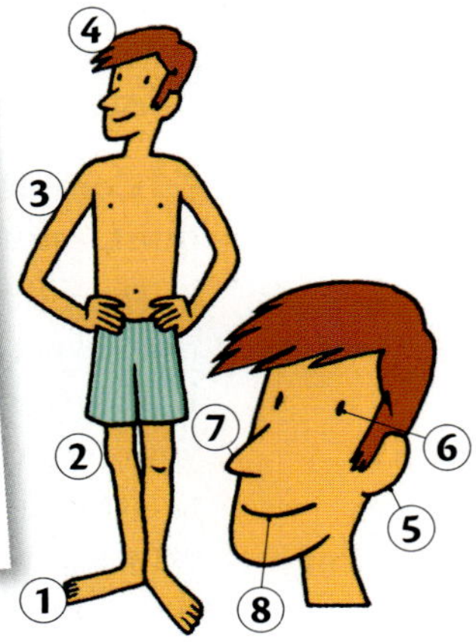

2 Associe l'adjectif avec le dessin qui lui correspond.

dangerous | beautiful | dark | scared | naughty

Practise your grammar

3 Voici quelques panneaux que l'on peut trouver à Westminster Abbey.
Explique leur signification en une phrase.

4 Regarde le plan ci-dessous et dis à ton ami ce qu'il doit faire pour aller de Green Park à Saint Luke's Church.

Practise your pronunciation

5 Écoute le début de la chanson et chante-le. Attention à bien prononcer l'auxiliaire *can*.

Can you touch your toes? (x2)
Yes, I can! Look at me! I can touch my toes!

Part 3

Check your progress

1 Listen

An interesting visit

ton objectif Comprendre la visite d'un château et la décrire.

There is/there are • Prépositions de lieu • *Must/mustn't* • Les prix.

Es-tu capable de :

A1
1. dire où se passe la visite, combien il y a de personnages, donner le prix de la visite ?

A2
2. expliquer ce qu'il faut ou ne faut pas faire pendant la visite ?
3. décrire la salle du château dont parle le guide ?

→ Go to your WB p. 56

2 Read

A great monument

ton objectif Comprendre l'essentiel d'une brochure touristique.

There is/there are • Le lexique lié aux monuments historiques.

Westminster Abbey

Adults £15.00
Schoolchildren (11-18 years) £6
Child under 11 free when accompanied by an adult
Open Monday – Saturday 9:30 a.m. – 4:30 p.m.

There are over one million visitors every year!
Westminster Abbey is in the heart of London – next to Big Ben and the Houses of Parliament. There are the tombs of English Kings and Queens including Queen Elizabeth I and her half-sister Bloody Mary!

Lis la brochure. Es-tu capable de :

A1
1. dire de quel monument il s'agit ?
2. situer le monument (ville, quartier) ?

A1+
3. parler des informations pratiques (prix, horaires) ?
4. dire si le monument est célèbre ?

→ Go to your WB p. 56

3 Speak

Meet the ghost!

ton objectif Imaginer et décrire un fantôme.

Have got • *Can/can't* • Les verbes d'action • Les parties du corps.

La Tour de Londres est hantée par les fantômes de nombreuses personnes qui y sont mortes. Imagine l'un d'entre eux, décris-le et présente-le à tes camarades qui te poseront des questions pour avoir plus de précisions.

Es-tu capable de :

A1
1. donner des informations sur son identité : nom et âge ?
2. décrire physiquement le fantôme ?

A1+
3. décrire ce qu'il est capable de faire ou pas ?
4. réagir et de répondre aux questions de tes camarades ?

→ Go to your WB p. 57

4 Write

A haunted castle

ton objectif Créer la brochure d'un château hanté imaginaire.

There is/there are • *Must/mustn't* • Les prix • Le lexique lié aux monuments historiques.

Nombre de mots 25

Rédige quelques lignes pour la brochure touristique d'un château anglais réputé hanté.

Es-tu capable de :

A1
1. donner des informations pratiques (prix, horaires) ?

A1+
2. décrire ce qu'il y a à visiter dans le château ?

A2
3. expliquer ce qu'il faut et ne faut pas faire pendant la visite du château ?

→ Go to your WB p. 57

Discovery

Have fun in London!

There's a tour for everyone!

Boat tour on the Thames

Have fun on the River Thames and see some of the most famous monuments in London including Big Ben!

Price (ticket valid all day): **£12.50**

The London Eye

On the way to Buckingham Palace

Bus tour

Visit the city on a famous London bus. Sightseeing tickets are valid all day and cost £25. Get on and off any time at over 90 different places!
Try stop n°32: it's Westminster Abbey, the most famous abbey in London.

The Royal West Bike tour

Explore the city on a bike with a professional guide!
Price: £18.95
The tour starts at Gabriel's Wharf on the River Thames and includes the London Eye, Saint James's Park and Buckingham Palace.

Did you know?

Buckingham Palace is the Queen's castle in London. There are 775 rooms (78 bathrooms!), 1,514 doors and 760 windows.

Buckingham Palace

Quiz time

Read and answer the questions.

1. Look at the map and say what monuments you can see with the boat tour.
2. Look at the map and give 6 monuments you would like to visit in London.
3. Give the names of two parks in London.
4. Mr and Mrs Perry would like to take the Bus Tour to visit London. How much is it?

FINAL TASK

Make up the programme of a two-day tour of London for year 7 pupils.

1. Choose the places of interest. Find information about them, say why they are interesting: what there is to see, what people can do, times, prices, location.
2. Use the map to make up the itinerary.
3. Give instructions to say what the pupils must and mustn't bring with them, what they must and mustn't do during the visits.

http://www.woodlands-junior.kent.sch.uk/customs/questions/regions/london.htm

Part 4 Family fun

My crazy family

CD ÉLÈVE PISTE 9 — Karaoké

There's my mother with green hair
But my father doesn't care.
There's my brother who gets stronger
Every breakfast, lunch and dinner
And my sister, oh yucky!
Who eats nothing but jelly!
What a strange and crazy family!
[...]
But my favourite one of all
Is my crazy uncle Paul.
Always sings, makes us fly
Always jumps and jumps so high
Often eats a dozen eggs
Always drinks two gallons straight!
Mister Crazy in the family!
[...]
Mother, father, brother, sister
Uncle, aunt, cousins together
Yes, I love, my crazy family
Yes, I love, my crazy, crazy, crazy family!

Unit 7 What a family!

Je vais m'entraîner à

- Comprendre des informations sur les goûts, les activités et le quotidien de quelqu'un.
- Comprendre un emploi du temps.
- Présenter l'emploi du temps de quelqu'un, ses activités et ses habitudes.
- Me renseigner sur la vie quotidienne, les activités et les goûts de quelqu'un.
- Préparer des questions pour un sondage et décrire le quotidien, les goûts et les activités de quelqu'un.

Je vais utiliser

Le présent simple (2) .... p. 69

Les adverbes de fréquence.... p. 69

Le lexique lié à la famille, aux habitudes de vie, à la nourriture. L'expression de l'heure.

→ Go to your WB p. 58

Discover

1 **Look at Andrew's family tree.**

a) Listen and repeat. Then match the words with the names in the tree.

grandfather
grandmother
grandparents
mother
father
parents
uncle
aunt
cousin
brother
sister

You: His grandfather is...

b) Listen for more information and speak about Andrew's family.
Pupil A: Who is his grandfather? What does he do?
Pupil B: His grandfather is...

Wordgym → Go to your WB p. 59

2 **Mrs Stickler and her family!**

a) Listen and speak about the Sticklers' everyday life.

b) Listen to the following sentences and say if they are true or false.
Ex.: The Sticklers live in London.
You: No, they don't. They live in a village called Grendon.

c) Now, play a memory game.
Pupil A: What time do... ? What do they have for breakfast?
Pupil B: For breakfast, they...

→ Go to your WB p. 59

3 **Listen to these sentences and say how many groups of words you can hear.**

Listen and speak

CD ÉLÈVE PISTE 10

4 a) Listen to the conversation and speak about Chad's plans and about the characters' hobbies and life habits.

b) Go to your WB p. 60

Tactics

Repère les mots de la même famille, ils te permettront de mieux comprendre les différentes informations entendues.

Words to remember

CD CLASSE

- aunt
- **bro**ther
- **fa**ther
- **heal**thy
- **mo**ther
- or**ga**nic food
- **sis**ter
- **un**cle
- a vege**ta**rian

Don't forget!

1. Le présent simple (2)

She sometimes eats eggs.
My parents never eat crisps.

2. La prononciation du « s » au présent simple

he eats – she plays – she watches

Go to your WB p. 61

QUICK CHECK → WB p. 64

Use what you know

5 Speak in pairs

Look at the information about Mr Green's life. Speak about his hobbies. What do you think of his lifestyle?

Pupil A: On Mondays, Mr Green …
Pupil B: I think Mr Green's lifestyle is … because…

6 Speak for a minute

CD CLASSE

a) Listen to Drake, and speak about his everyday life.
b) Listen and sing the "Vampire Song".

He's always up around midnight
He never sleeps during the night…
Watch! The Vampire comes!

Go to your WB p. 62

YOUR TASK

7 Make a survey about your friends' lifestyle and hobbies.

1. Prepare your questions (typical school day, hobbies…)
   You: What time do you… ? Do you play… ? Do you go… ?
2. Question your friends. Collect your answers in a grid *(tableau)*.
3. Use the answers to write a paragraph about your friends' life.

B2i Make a grid with a computer.

Video Flash DVD

This is my family

Grammar

Le présent simple (2)

→ On utilise le présent simple pour parler de ses **habitudes de vie**.

Forme affirmative	Forme négative	Forme interrogative
*I **get up** at 9 o'clock.* *He **gets up** at 8 o'clock.*	*I **don't drink** soda.* *He **doesn't eat** hamburgers.*	***Do** you **play** football?* ***Does** he **play** basket ball?*

⚠ N'oublie pas les changements à la **troisième personne du singulier** (she / he / it) :
- à la forme affirmative, on ajoute **« -s »** à la base verbale ou **« -es »** après les verbes se terminant par -o, -ch, -sh.
  *He get**s** up. He go**es**. He watch**es**.*
- à la forme négative, ***doesn't*** remplace ***don't***.
  *He **doesn't** eat sweets.*
- à la forme interrogative, ***does*** remplace ***do***.
  ***Does** she play the piano ?*

Les adverbes de fréquence

→ Tu utilises les adverbes de fréquence pour dire si tu fais une action parfois (***sometimes***), souvent (***often***), toujours (***always***) ou jamais (***never***).

→ L'adverbe de fréquence se place toujours **devant le verbe**, mais **après** l'auxiliaire ***be***.

*Does he **often** play rugby?*
*My parents **never** eat hamburgers.*
*They are **always** happy.*
*She **sometimes** drinks tomato juice.*

Exercises

1 Complète ces phrases avec *do, does, don't* ou *doesn't*. Traduis-les en français.

a. She … play the piano. She plays the guitar.
b. … you get up at 8 o'clock every day?
c. … he play rugby every Saturday?
d. I … eat hamburgers. I think they are not healthy.
e. He … drink alcohol.

2 Remets les éléments dans l'ordre pour faire des phrases. Traduis-les en français.

a. often/cinema/to/I/go/the
b. they/science-fiction films/watch/never
c. gets up/always/Tom/8 o'clock/at
d. do/Saturday/tennis/every/play/you/?
e. Andrew/rugby/plays/on/sometimes/Wednesdays

3 Dis si tu fais ces actions parfois, souvent, tout le temps ou jamais. Rédige des phrases complètes.

a. go to the museum
b. go to the cinema
c. watch romantic films
d. eat organic food
e. drink sodas and eat sweets

More exercises → p. 154
CD ÉLÈVE Audio-Rom

ENGLISH LAB — La prononciation du « s » au présent simple

CD CLASSE

1 Écoute ces phrases.

*She sometimes **eats** eggs. She **plays** the guitar.*
*Mr. Stickler **watches** television every day.*

Le « –s » final se prononce de trois façons différentes.

/s/	/z/	/iz/
eats, drinks	*plays, sings*	*watches*

2 Lis ces phrases à voix haute en tenant compte de la bonne prononciation du « s ».

a. Mrs. Stickler always washes dishes after dinner.
b. Chad's aunt plays the guitar all the time.
c. Mrs. O'Malley thinks her sister sings very well.
d. Chad's mother only eats vegetables and always drinks tomato juice.

More exercises →
CD ÉLÈVE Audio-Rom

Language practice

Practise your **vocabulary**

1 Les mots suivants se rapportent au thème de la famille. Les lettres ont été mélangées. Remets-les dans l'ordre. Puis traduis en français.

c n e l u — h r b o t r e

r g n a f d t a e h r — t n u a

h o m t e r — r h e t o d m n a r g

h t f a r e — u c o n i s

t s s i r e

2 Rappelle-toi l'histoire « What a family! » et complète les phrases suivantes avec l'adverbe de fréquence qui convient (*sometimes, often, never, always*).

a. Chad's parents … eat crisps.
b. His mother … drinks tomato juice.
c. His mother … eats eggs.
d. Tom … plays rugby on Saturdays.
e. Chad's mother … says: "An apple a day keeps the doctor away".

Practise your **grammar**

3 Regarde cet extrait de l'emploi du temps de Matt.

Monday 10 a.m.: tennis
Tuesday 3 p.m.: piano
Wednesday 12.30: lunch
Friday 3 p.m.: back home
Saturday: swimming

Réponds aux questions suivantes.

a. What does he do on Tuesdays at 3 p.m.?
b. What time does he play tennis on Mondays?
c. What time does he have lunch on Wednesdays?
d. What time does he go home on Fridays?
e. What sport does he do on Saturdays?

4 Réponds aux questions suivantes selon ton propre emploi du temps.

a. What time do you get up on schooldays?
b. What time do you go to bed on schooldays? At the weekend?
c. What do you often have for breakfast?
d. What time do you have lunch on schooldays?
e. Do you eat at school or at home?
f. What sports do you do? When?
g. What do you often do at the weekend?

Practise your **pronunciation**

CD CLASSE

5 Écoute et classe les mots dans le tableau en fonction de la prononciation du « s » final.

eats — stops — watches — continues — plays — drinks — washes — surprises

/s/	/z/	/ɪz/
…	…	…

Unit 8 A picnic in Canterbury

Je vais m'entraîner à

- Comprendre à qui appartient un objet.
- Comprendre un « *chant* » au sujet de la nourriture.
- Dire à qui appartient telle ou telle chose.
- Me renseigner sur l'appartenance de tel ou tel objet.
- Écrire les répliques d'un dialogue.

Je vais utiliser

Whose et le génitif..... p. 75

Les articles .... p. 75

Le lexique de la nourriture.
→ Go to your WB p. 58

Discover

1 It is important to eat healthy food.
Read the words below and say if you think it is healthy or not.

vegetables | hamburgers | soda | sweets
fruit | milk | ketchup | chips | fish | crisps
grilled meat | alcohol | fruit juice

You: I think chips are…

Wordgym → Go to your WB p. 65

2 Getting ready for the picnic! Look at the drawing. Then listen to Tom and his mother and say:

a. why Tom's mother is not happy.
b. what there is in the picnic basket.
c. whose things they are.

→ Go to your WB p. 65

3 Listen to the intonation and say if the voice goes up or down at the end of the sentences.

"A teddy bear?"
"And these keys?"
"And this mobile phone?" (…)

"A teddy bear!"
"And these keys!"
"And this mobile phone!"

Listen and speak

CD ÉLÈVE PISTE 11

4 **Listen carefully. First, speak about the problems during the picnic and then speak about the boys' adventures in the cathedral.**

→ Go to your WB p. 66

Tactics

Concentre-toi sur l'intonation des phrases (descendante ou montante ?). Cela t'aidera à identifier le type de phrases (interrogative, affirmative ou exclamative) et te permettra de mieux comprendre une conversation.

Words to remember

CD CLASSE

- cheese
- ch**o**colate cake
- crisps
- ham
- **jell**y
- juice
- **sau**sages
- tom**a**to
- **ve**getables

Don't forget!

1. WHOSE et le génitif

Whose carrot juice is this?
This is Mr O'Malley's (carrot juice).

2. La prononciation de « p », « t », « c », « ch »

prince /prɪns/
tomato /tə'mɑːtəʊ/
cake /keɪk/ *chips* /ʧɪps/

→ Go to your WB p. 68

QUICK CHECK → WB p. 70

Use what you know

5 Speak for a minute

Listen carefully. Whose lunchbox is it?

You: This is...

6 Speak in pairs

Look at the objects below and challenge the class. Whose are they?

Use: Scarlett, Mrs O'Malley, Mr O'Malley, Chad's brother.

Pupil A: Whose... ?
Pupil B: I think... because...

YOUR TASK

7 Write a short dialogue and act it out.

Tom's family is going out on a picnic. Everything is in a mess. There are things everywhere, and Tom's mother is not very happy about it. She wants to organize things.

1. Make a list of the characters.
2. Make a list of Tom's mother's different problems.
3. Write the conversation.
4. Memorize it and act it out with your classmates.

Go to your WB p. 68

Video Flash DVD

Lost in Canterbury

Grammar

■ Le marqueur de possession

➜ Le « 's » placé entre le détenteur d'un objet et l'objet s'appelle le **génitif**. Il est utilisé pour dire **à qui appartient un objet**.

It's Mr. ***O'Malley's sandwich****.*

On emploie aussi **'s** pour les liens de parenté.

Zoe is ***Tom's sister****.*

⚠ Ne confonds pas avec les formes contractées suivantes : *Tom's English.* (=Tom is)

Tom's got a little sister. (=Tom has)

➜ Si le détenteur est au pluriel, le génitif se forme avec l'apostrophe sans le **s**.

The boys' adventures.

■ *Whose*

➜ On utilise le pronom interrogatif ***whose*** pour demander à qui appartient un objet.

Whose *hamburger is it?* ***Whose*** *keys are they?*

■ Les articles *a*/*an* et *the*

➜ L'article indéfini (un / une) se dit ***a*** en anglais. Il devient ***an*** quand le nom qui le suit commence par une voyelle.

a *hamburger* ***an*** *organic sandwich*

➜ Pour parler des choses en général, on n'utilise pas d'article (Ø = absence d'article) au singulier et au pluriel.

I love ø orange juice *I love ø cakes*

➜ L'article défini (le, la, les) se dit ***the*** en anglais. Il se prononce /ðiː/ quand le nom qui le suit commence par un son voyelle.

The dog (le chien) *The orange* (l'orange)

Exercises

1 Traduis en anglais

a. l'ami de Zoe
b. le sandwich de Mr O'Malley
c. la sœur de Tom
d. le téléphone de la mère de Chad
e. le stylo de Scarlett

2 Écoute les cinq questions et dis à chaque fois de quelle forme il s'agit : *Who's* ? ou *Whose* ? Puis traduis-les en français.

3 Pose les questions correspondant aux réponses ci-dessous.

a. It's Tom's house.
b. They are Mr O'Malley's keys.
c. It's my bag!
d. It's Zoe's bedroom.
e. It's her mobile phone.

4 Complète les phrases avec l'article qui convient.

a. Look! This is ... Cathedral of Canterbury.
b. I don't want ... fruit! I want ... hamburger.
c. ... apple ... day keeps ... doctor away.
d. It is ... famous monument. I love ... cathedrals.
e. ... hamburgers and ... sugar are not healthy.

More exercises ➜ p. 154

CD ÉLÈVE Audio-Rom

ENGLISH LAB CD CLASSE

La prononciation de « p », « t », « c », « ch »

1 Écoute ces mots.

Paul – **p**rince – **T**homas – **c**ake – **ch**ips

Tu remarques qu'en anglais, ces consonnes se prononcent plus fortement qu'en français quand elles sont en début de mot. Classe-les dans le tableau.

/p/	/t/	/k/	/tʃ/
...	...	...	...

2 Écoute et répète ces phrases en prononçant correctement les lettres « p », « t », « c », « ch »

a. Peter, Paul and Patrick always take chips and cake on their picnics.
b. Charles's chocolate chip cookies are perfect!

More exercises ➜

CD ÉLÈVE Audio-Rom

Language practice

Practise your vocabulary

1 a) Écoute le *chant* « *An apple a day* » et fais la liste des aliments qui y sont mentionnés. Puis répartis-les en deux colonnes : ceux qui sont recommandés et ceux qui ne le sont pas.

b) Répète et mémorise le *chant*.

An apple a day keeps the doctor away
We must eat fruit every day
Apples and carrots every day!
Burgers? Sandwiches? Crisps or chips?
No, no, no, no, no!
Fruit and veggies every day!
Tomatoes, oranges, kiwis and bananas
Oh yes!
An apple a day keeps the doctor away!

Practise your grammar

2 Recopie les phrases ci-dessous en remplaçant *'s* par *is* ou *has* quand cela est possible. Traduis-les en français.

a. John's got a great book on Canterbury Cathedral.
b. John's book's about Thomas Beckett and King Henry II.
c. Tom's excited because he's in Canterbury with Chad's family.
d. Paul's Chad's uncle. He's a little crazy but he's fun!
e. Chad's uncle's got a sister. Her name's Mary.

3 Regarde le dessin et fais quatre phrases pour expliquer quel aliment appartient à quel personnage.

4 Complète les phrases avec l'article qui convient : a / an / the / Ø

a. I always eat … apple in the morning.
b. … chocolate cake is my favourite dessert.
c. I would like … crisps and … hamburger, please.
d. I love … cathedrals, but … Cathedral of Canterbury is my favourite !
e. Look! There is … piece of … chocolate cake on … table!

HAVE FUN

5 Écoute et répète ce poème.

What a mess!
Poor Tom's room is in a mess!
On his desk, there's Zoe's dress
On his bed, there's Zoe's bear
And Zoe's toys, under his chair!
Poor Tom's room is in a mess!
His sister's things are everywhere!

Practise your pronunciation

6 Écoute et répète la phrase suivante en prononçant correctement les consonnes soulignées.

Paul, Patrick, Chad and Tom chat on their computer every Tuesday night.

Part 4

Unit 9 We had a great time!

Je vais m'entraîner à

- Comprendre le récit d'une excursion.
- Comprendre un message racontant les événements du week-end.
- Présenter ce que quelqu'un a fait lors d'une excursion.
- Me renseigner sur ce que quelqu'un a fait pendant le week-end.
- Écrire un e-mail pour raconter ce que l'on a fait lors d'une visite à Londres.

Je vais utiliser

Le prétérit de *be* (1) .... p. 81

Le prétérit (2) des verbes lexicaux... p. 81

Le lexique de la ville.

→ Go to your WB p. 58

Discover

1 Look at the map and listen to the description of the town. Match the numbers with the words below.

Ex.: In Bank Street, there is a bookshop next to the bar.

(5) → a bookshop.

- a bookshop
- a restaurant
- a hotel
- a church
- a supermarket
- a bakery
- a butcher
- a cinema
- a pub
- the post office
- the swimming-pool

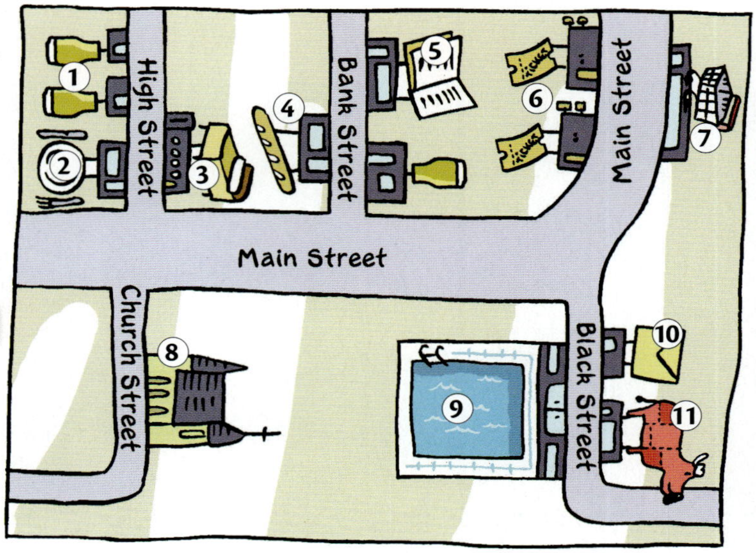

Wordgym → Go to your WB p. 71

2 A great visit!

a) Listen and say where Matt and Jodie were yesterday.

b) What did they do?

c) Did they like their visit?

→ Go to your WB p. 71

3 Read the document and say what sort of document it is. Justify your answer.

From: chadomalley@hotmail.uk

To: tom.spencer@hotmail.uk

Hi, Tom!

You know what? Things are a little difficult at home today ☹ : there's uncle Paul in hospital and my Mum is mad at my sister because she bought a hamburger on the way back home this afternoon! So I'm afraid I can't come and play video games with you tonight! ☹ ☹ What about next Saturday? 😉

CU! Chad

Read and speak

4 **Look at the document and say what it is.**
Who wrote it? To whom?
Read it carefully and say what it is about.

→ Go to your WB p. 72

Tactics

Utilise tous les indices présents sur un document écrit pour en comprendre rapidement la nature, pour comprendre qui s'adresse à qui, ainsi que le sujet général abordé.

From: scarlettwilliams@myworld.com
To: kevinwilliams@yahoo.com
Subject: A crazy weekend

Dear Dad,

I had a very strange week end. On Saturday, Chad invited me to a picnic party with his family. We went to Canterbury. His family is a bit strange! His mother ate carrots and drank tomato juice! I didn't eat carrots!! I had crisps 🙂. Chad's uncle, Paul, said there was some treasure in the cathedral. The treasure of the Black Prince. He wanted to find it. So, Paul, Chad and Tom went to explore the cathedral. They didn't find any treasure, but they saw the Black Prince's tomb and the place where Thomas Beckett was executed. They decided to go down into the crypt, but Paul fell down the stairs and he broke his leg! 🙁 We called an ambulance. The ambulance took Paul to the hospital! It was a crazy day with a crazy family but we had fun! It was a great day! And you? How are you? How is everything in New York? Did you have a nice weekend? Did you go to Central Park? Please write soon. I miss you.

Love,

Scarlett.

Words to remember

CD CLASSE

- break → broke
- call → called
- decide → decided
- drink → drank
- eat → ate
- explore → explored
- find → found
- go → went
- have → had
- invite → invited
- take → took
- want → wanted

Don't forget!

1. Le prétérit (1)

I was... She was... We were...
I played... I ate / I didn't play... I didn't eat...
Did you go to Central Park?

2. La prononciation de la terminaison *-ed*

played /d/ – watched /t/ – wanted /ɪd/

→ Go to your WB p. 74

QUICK CHECK → WB p. 76

Use what you know

5 Speak for a minute

Yesterday, John and Linda were in Oxford.

Look at the pictures. Listen and say if the sentences are true or false and why.

You: No, they weren't. Yesterday at 1 p. m., they were in a church.

6 Speak in pairs

a) **The class interviews a pupil about his past weekend.**

b) **Collect the information and then recap orally.**

Class: What did you... ? Did you...?
Pupil: I went... Yes, I did / No, I didn't.

→ Go to your WB p. 74

YOUR TASK

7 Write an email about a visit to London.

Imagine you went to London at the weekend.
You write an email to your best friend about your visit.

1. Say what time you arrived, where and what you ate, what monuments you visited.
2. When did you eat? Give precise times.
3. Say what you liked, what you didn't like.

Grammar

Le prétérit de *be*

➜ L'auxiliaire **be**

Be au présent	***Be*** au prétérit (forme affirmative)	***Be*** au prétérit (forme négative)
I ***am*** *You* ***are*** *She / He / It* ***is*** *We* ***are*** *They* ***are***	*I* ***was*** *You* ***were*** *She / He / It* ***was*** *We* ***were*** *They* ***were***	*I* ***wasn't*** *You* ***weren't*** *She / He / It* ***wasn't*** *We* ***weren't*** *They* ***weren't***

➜ À la forme interrogative, comme au présent, l'auxiliaire ***be*** passe devant le sujet.

Is he at school? *Was he at school?*

Le prétérit des verbes autres que *be*

➜ Tous les verbes en anglais n'ont qu'une **seule forme au passé à toutes les personnes**.

➜ **À la forme affirmative**, il suffit d'ajouter ***-ed*** à la base verbale.

play ➜ *I played* (J'ai joué)

Certains verbes ne suivent pas cette règle et ont une forme passée différente. On dit que ces verbes sont irréguliers, car ils ne suivent pas la règle du ***-ed***.

➜ **À la forme négative**, il suffit d'ajouter ***didn't*** devant la base verbale, et ceci pour tous les verbes.

I ***didn't play*** *tennis.* *I* ***didn't go*** *to London.*

➜ **À la forme interrogative**, il suffit d'utiliser l'auxiliaire ***did*** à toutes les personnes.

Did *you play tennis yesterday?*
Where ***did*** *she go during her weekend?*

Exercises

1 Complète les phrases avec *was* ou *were*. Traduis les phrases en français.

a. John … in London with his friend yesterday.
b. Tom and Chad … very happy to visit the Cathedral.
c. The columns in the Cathedral … very big.
d. I … in Westminster Abbey in August. It … very beautiful.
e. We … at the cinema yesterday afternoon.

2 Conjugue les verbes des phrases suivantes au prétérit. Traduis les phrases en français.

a. We (*invite*) Sophie and Jack to the restaurant.
b. They (*go*) to London and Oxford in January.
c. I (*want*) to visit the Tower of London. But it (*be*) closed.
d. John (*go*) to the restaurant. He (*eat*) chips and a hamburger. He (*drink*) Coke.
e. In Canterbury Cathedral, John and Chad (*find*) the Black Prince's statue.

3 Toutes ces phrases sont fausses. Réécris-les à la forme négative.

a. Jack was in New York in September.
b. Sophie and Patrick ate in a restaurant yesterday.
c. Fred played video games with his friend.
d. I wanted to go to the cinema yesterday.
e. They drank carrot and tomato juice.

More exercises ➜ p. 154 CD ÉLÈVE Audio-Rom

ENGLISH LAB La prononciation de la terminaison « *-ed* ».

CD CLASSE

1 Écoute ces trois verbes :

I played – I danced – I decided

La terminaison ***-ed*** se prononce de trois façons différentes :

/d/	/t/	/ɪd/
comme dans *played*	comme dans *danced*	quand le verbe se termine par le son /t/ ou /d/ comme dans *decided – wanted – started*

2 Écoute et répète ces phrases à voix haute. Attention à la prononciation de *-ed*.

a. I watched a good film yesterday.
b. We decided to visit Canterbury Cathedral.
c. They played video games all afternoon.
d. They danced all night with friends.

More exercises ➜ CD ÉLÈVE Audio-Rom

Language practice

Practise your **vocabulary**

1 Fais correspondre chaque dessin à un nom de lieu dans la ville en fonction de la définition que tu entends.

2 Lis le texte ci-dessous et retrouve les verbes qui manquent. Conjugue-les au passé.

Yesterday, I . . . to London with my parents. We . . . the Tower of London. It . . . great! We . . . to a restaurant. I . . . a hamburger and I . . . Coke. In the afternoon, we . . . to the cinema. We . . . Avatar. It . . . a good film!

Practise your **grammar**

3 Écoute le poème et répète-le.

a. Recopie les verbes du poème et classe-les dans un tableau (verbes réguliers / verbes irréguliers) en précisant à chaque fois l'infinitif et la traduction en français.
b. Recopie le poème et illustre les scènes.
c. Écoute les affirmations et dis si elles sont vraies ou fausses.
Justifie ta réponse.

A rat and a cat

A rat and a cat went out one day
They walked to the park, then started to play
And they laughed and had fun
They decided to run
And they ran, and they ran
All the way to Japan!
There they stopped near a tree
And had two cups of tea!
And they saw Snook, the snake!
And they ate a big cake.
And they played, and they played
And they danced, and they danced.
Oh! They wanted to stay
Till the end of the day.
But it was time to run
And go back to Britain!

Practise your **pronunciation**

4 Écoute à nouveau le poème et classe les verbes en fonction de la prononciation de la terminaison *-ed*.

/t/	/d/	/ɪd/
...	...	...

Part 4

Check your progress

1 Listen

Lost and found

ton objectif Écouter et dire à qui appartient telle ou telle chose.

Whose • Le génitif.

Écoute attentivement la conversation.
Es-tu capable de :

- A1 — 1. dire où se passe la scène, combien il y a de personnages ?
- A1 — 2. dire de quels objets l'on parle ?
- A1+ — 3. repérer à qui appartient chaque objet mentionné ?

→ Go to your WB p. 78

2 Read

Dover Castle

ton objectif Comprendre le récit d'une excursion sur une carte postale.

Le prétérit • Le lexique lié aux monuments historiques.

Canterbury, June 3rd, 2010.

Dear Mum and Dad,

I'm still in Canterbury. Yesterday, I went to Dover with Uncle Harry and Aunt Jenny. We visited Dover Castle. It was very interesting. We saw a nice church. We stayed four hours at the castle. Inside the castle, there were things about King Henry VIII. At lunch time, we had a picnic. We ate sandwiches and drank sodas. We had a really good time! But Uncle Harry had a little problem! He didn't see a large stone and he fell down! But fortunately, he didn't break his leg! It was a fun day!

Sam

Lis attentivement la carte postale.
Es-tu capable de :

- A1 — 1. dire qui a écrit la carte et à qui elle est adressée ?
- A1+ — 2. dire brièvement ce dont on parle dans la carte postale ?
- A2 — 3. décrire en détail les événements racontés dans la carte postale ?

→ Go to your WB p. 78

3 Speak

A businessman's life

ton objectif Parler des activités et des habitudes de quelqu'un.

Le présent simple • L'heure.

Voici la journée typique d'un homme d'affaires, Mr Duncan.
Décris sa vie quotidienne.

6:00 Get up
6:30 Breakfast
8:00 Work
12:00 Lunch
2:00 Meetings
8:00 Home
9:00 Dinner
10:00 Bed

Es-tu capable de :

- A1 — 1. donner des informations sur son identité : nom, métier ?
- A1+ — 2. décrire avec des phrases simples quelques activités de Mr Duncan ?
- A2 — 3. décrire en détail les activités de Mr Duncan, en en précisant les heures, et en reliant les phrases avec *and* ou *but* ?

→ Go to your WB p. 79

4 Write

A day in Canterbury

ton objectif Écrire une carte postale.

Le prétérit.

Tu es allé(e) à Canterbury pour une journée.
Tu rédiges une carte postale pour tes parents.

Es-tu capable de :

- A1 — 1. présenter correctement la carte postale ?
- A1+ — 2. écrire quelques phrases sur Canterbury ?
- A2 — 3. décrire en détail ce que tu as fait, les monuments que tu as visités, ce que tu as mangé et où ? dire si tu as aimé ou pas ?

→ Go to your WB p. 79

Discovery

The British Royal Family

Hello!
I am Prince William, Queen Elizabeth II's grandson. I was born on the 21st of June, 1982. I have got one brother. His name is Harry. I've got one dog named Widgeon. He is a Labrador born in 2005. For food, I like pasta, hamburgers, chocolate, venison, fruit salad and eggs from my father's organic farm. I like fast cars. I like sports and painting. I want to become a rescue pilot in the RAF (Royal Air Force).

This is my family

Queen Elizabeth II (1926) ♥ Prince Philip (1921)

Prince Charles (1948) — Princess Anne (1950) — Prince Andrew (1960) — Prince Edward (1964)

Prince Charles: Diana (1961-1997) · Camilla (1947)

Prince William (1982) — Prince Harry (1984)

Queen Mum

(Born on August 4, 1900 – Died on March 30, 2002)
She was my great grandmother. Everyone loved her! She was very popular! She died when she was 101 years old.

Favourite food: *Herrings, English muffins, salmon sandwiches.*

Hobbies: *Gardening (growing Camelias), reading.*

Queen Elizabeth

My grandmother, Queen Elizabeth was born on the 21 April 1926. She became Queen in 1952.

Homes: *Buckingham Palace, London. Windsor Castle. Balmoral, Scotland.*

Favourite food: *Traditional British food including roast beef, Yorkshire pudding, roast potatoes and vegetables. Organic food from her son's organic farm.*

Hobbies: *Animals (horses, dogs). Walking in the forest. Scottish dances.*

Everyday life: *Attending important ceremonies. Reading and answering letters. Meeting with important people. Supporting 620 charities.*

Prince Charles

My father, Prince Charles was born on November 14, 1948 in Buckingham Palace.
Favourite food: *Traditional British food. Good Whisky. Only organic food. He founded a company called Duchy. They only produce organic food. (http://www.duchyoriginals.com/)*
Favourite place: *Scotland.*
Hobbies: *Sports, hunting, shooting, fishing, polo, skiing, painting, writing and reading.*

Prince Harry

He is my brother. He was born on September 15, 1984.
Hobbies: *Charity work, military activities, football, rugby, polo, skiing, tennis, hunting.*

Princess Diana

(Born on 1 July 1961 – Died on 31 August 1997, aged 36) She was my mother. Harry and I loved her a lot. We were very close. She died in Paris in a car accident.
Husband: *Charles, Prince of Wales (29 July 1981 – divorced on 28 August 1996).*
Children: *Prince William of Wales, Prince Henry of Wales.*

Quiz time

Read and answer the questions.

1. Give the names of Prince William's uncles.
2. Who is Princess Anne?
3. What is William's dog's name? How old is he?
4. What is William's favourite food? Hobbies?
5. When did Queen Elizabeth become Queen of England?

FINAL TASK

Create an illustrated poster of the British Royal Family tree.

1. On a large sheet of paper, reproduce the Royal family tree. You must find information about the Queen's parents and add them to the tree.
2. Choose three members of the Royal Family. Use the information on this page to write a paragraph about their lives, hobbies and occupations.
3. Display your paragraphs around the family tree.

http://www.royal.gov.uk/

Part 5 Show time

It's show time

CD ÉLÈVE PISTE 12 Karaoké

I'm walking down the avenue
I'm all alone and thinking of you!
Feeling better, feeling great!
Yes you're my star and I can't wait!
The night is clear, the night is bright
Not out of mind, not out of sight!
I feel the colors in my heart
We're not alone, we're not apart!

Chorus
Are you coming to meet me?
Are you saying you are free?
Are you coming to see me?
We love the night!
It's *show time*!
We're singing! We are dancing!
We are jumping! We are running!

Clap your hands! The fun is here!
Clap your hands! Let us all cheer!
It's *Show time*! It's *Show time*!
We all love the night!!
It's *Show time*! It's *Show time*!
We all , we all, we all.... love the night!!

Unit 10 Time to act

Je vais m'entraîner à

- Comprendre les arguments d'un candidat pendant une audition.
- Identifier les personnages dans un récit.
- Comparer deux personnes entre elles.
- Choisir un candidat et justifier mon choix.
- Décrire ses qualités pour un rôle.

Je vais utiliser

Le comparatif...... p. 91

Le lexique des émotions et des sentiments.

→ Go to your WB p. 80

Discover

1 Can you describe someone?

a) Listen to the adjectives and repeat them.
b) Now, listen to the riddles (*devinettes*) and guess who is who.

James Bond

Catwoman

Laurel and Hardy

Snow White

Wordgym → Go to your WB p. 81

2 Jackson Jones, a film director, is speaking about his favourite actors. Listen and say who is who.

You: I think number 1 is... because...

→ Go to your WB p. 81

3 Listen to the characters and pick out the stressed words. What words can you hear the most?

Listen and speak

CD ÉLÈVE PISTE 13

4 **a) Look at the first picture and react. Who can you see? How are they feeling?**

b) → Go to your WB p. 82

Tactics

Les mots prononcés de façon plus marquée que les autres correspondent à des informations essentielles dans le message.

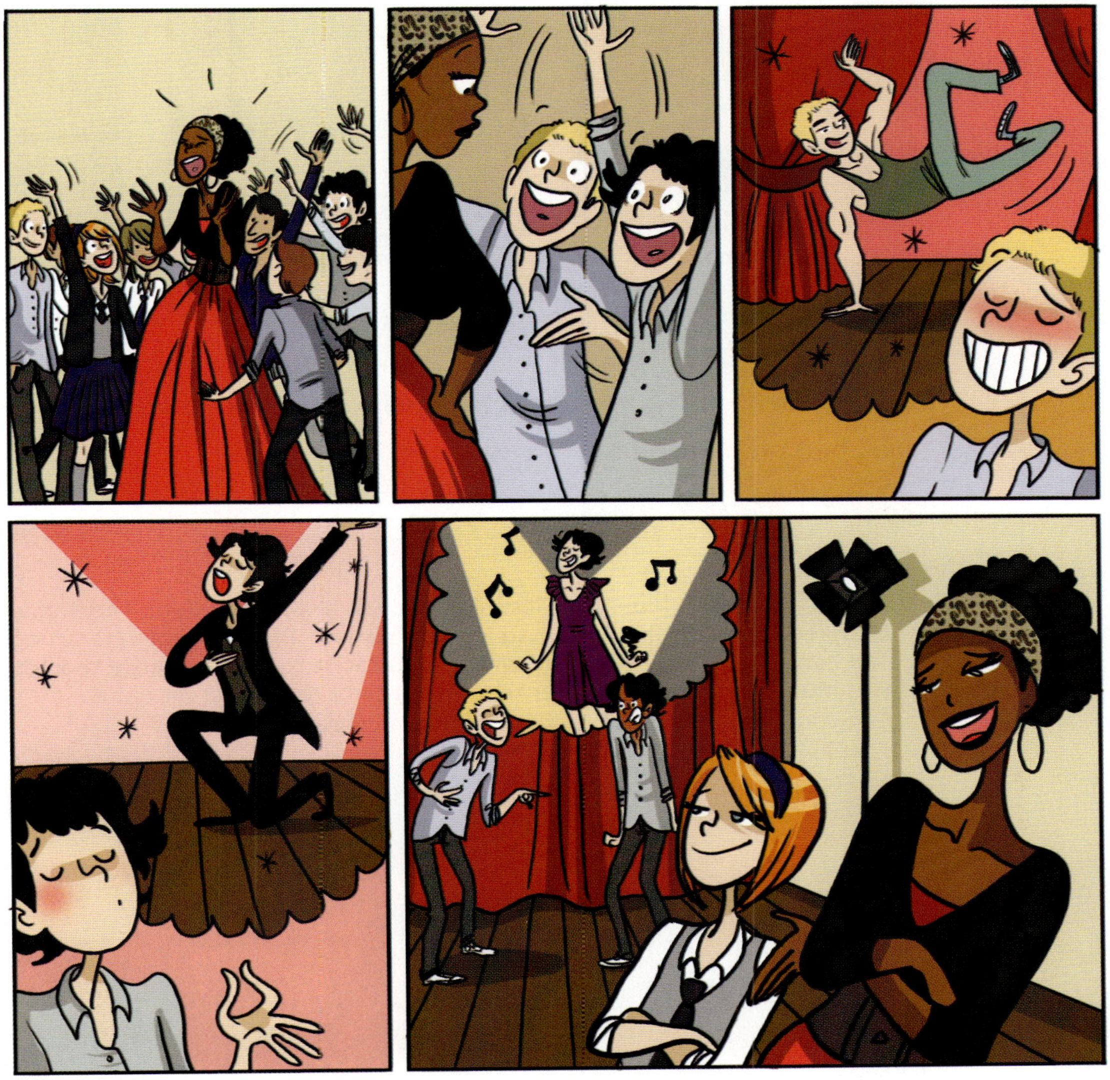

Words to remember

CD CLASSE

- ath**le**tic
- at**trac**tive
- **fun**ny
- **good-look**ing
- **hard-work**ing
- in**tel**ligent
- senti**men**tal
- strong
- tall

Don't forget!

1. Le comparatif de supériorité

Chad is funnier.
Tom works harder.

2. Le suffixe « er »

better – **tall**er – **strong**er

→ Go to your WB p. 83

QUICK CHECK → WB p. 86

Use what you know

5 Speak in pairs

Choose your favourite hero. Discuss with your classmates: say which hero you prefer and why.

Spiderman

Harry Potter

Troy

6 Speak for a minute

Read this email and guess who it is about. Justify your answer.

You: I think's it's… because…

Hi,
I saw a very funny film on TV last night! It was a village in Gaul. The Romans attacked them but the Gauls had a magic potion! They were always stronger! The hero was a very small man with a moustache but my favourite character was much bigger and stronger than him! I can't remember his name…
Can you give me the name of my favourite character?
Thanks.
Matt

→ Go to your WB p. 84

YOUR TASK

7 Audition for a role.

1. Read this ad.

> **ACTORS AND ACTRESSES WANTED**
> for a new Broadway show "Pirates of the Carribbean: the musical". Candidates must be very athletic, have a good memory and be very sensitive.

2. Prepare your arguments: write down your qualities for the role.
3. Audition in pairs. Explain why you are better than your partner.

→ Go to your WB p. 84

Video Flash DVD

At the drama club

Grammar

Le comparatif

Tu utilises le comparatif pour **comparer deux objets ou deux personnes**.

➜ La formation du comparatif

Adjectif	Comparatif
Adjectif d'**une syllabe** ou de **2 syllabes terminées par une voyelle** *tall*	**-er** *taller*
Adjectifs de **2 syllabes (terminées par une consonne) ou plus** *athletic*	**more** + adj ***more** athletic*

⚠ Attention ! Il peut y avoir des changements orthographiques et des cas irréguliers :

– quand un adjectif d'**une syllabe** se termine par une voyelle et une consonne, on double la consonne.

big → bigger *fat → fatter*

– quand un adjectif de **deux syllabes** se termine par « y », le « y » devient « i » et est suivi de **-er**.

funny → funnier *pretty → prettier*

➜ Les comparatifs irréguliers.

*good → **better*** *bad → **worse***

➜ La construction du comparatif.
Lorsque deux objets ou personnes comparés apparaissent dans la même phrase, le deuxième est introduit par la conjonction **than**.

*Chad is taller **than** Tom.*
*Tom is a better actor **than** Chad.*

Exercises

1 Mets l'adjectif entre parenthèses au comparatif de supériorité.

a. Tom is (+ intelligent) than Brad.
b. Lucy is (+ athletic) than Mary.
c. Chocolate is (+ good) than toffee.
d. Spiderman is (+ sentimental) than James Bond.
e. Tom is a bad actor but Chad is (+ bad).

2 Rédige cinq questions sur Tom et Jerry en utilisant le comparatif de supériorité.

Ex.: Who is bigger?

3 Compare les éléments suivants entre eux en utilisant l'adjectif donné.

a. Chad / Tom (funny)
b. Australia / France (big)
c. Planes / trains (fast)
d. Tigers / cats (strong)
e. Einstein / Donald Duck (intelligent)

More exercises ➜ p. 154 CD ÉLÈVE Audio-Rom

ENGLISH LAB CD CLASSE Le suffixe « -er »

1 Écoute et répète les mots suivants.

faster – better – taller – funnier – stronger

2 Que remarques-tu au sujet de la lettre « r » finale ?

3 Lis les phrases suivantes à voix haute.

a. The more, the merrier.
b. This car is faster and it looks better.
c. That car is smaller, but it's cheaper.

More exercises ➜ CD ÉLÈVE Audio-Rom

Language practice

Practise your vocabulary

1 Les espaces ont été oubliés. Retrouve les 10 adjectifs cachés ici et recopie-les dans ton cahier.

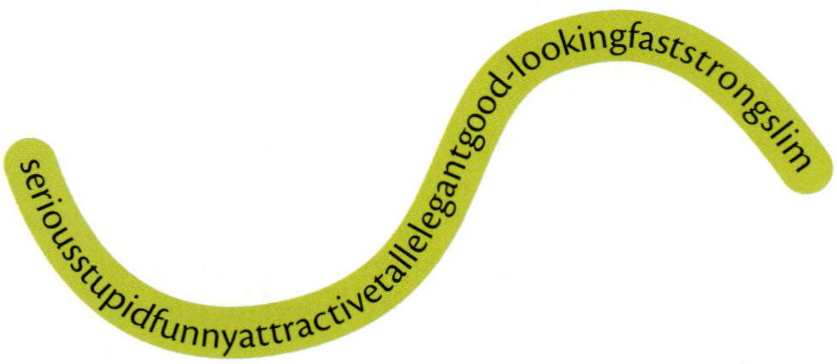

2 Recopie ces phrases en complétant avec l'adjectif qui convient.

a. He can run 10 kilometres in 30 minutes: he's very f...!
b. She's a very beautiful woman: she's very a...
c. This boy never laughs: he's very s...
d. She loves romantic films and love stories: she's very s...

3 Retrouve l'intrus dans chaque liste.

a. beautiful – ugly – attractive – good-looking
b. big – tall – small – high
c. fast – quick – athletic – slow
d. stupid – smart – clever – intelligent

Practise your grammar

4 Retrouve le mot qui manque dans chaque phrase.

a. The red car is faster ... the green one.
b. I think John is ... intelligent than Mark.
c. Which country is ...? Mexico or the U.S.A?
d. I prefer this actor: I think he's ... attractive.
e. Do you think that lions are stronger ... tigers?

5 Trouve les réponses à ces devinettes.

a. I'm longer than a minute but shorter than a day. What am I?
b. I'm shorter than a kilometer but longer than a centimetre. What am I?
c. I'm older than my brother but younger than my sister. Am I my parents' first, second or third child?

Practise your pronunciation

CD CLASSE

HAVE FUN **6 Entraîne-toi à répéter ce « tongue-twister ».**

Brad's funnier and stronger but John's a better actor.

Unit 11 Get ready for the show

Je vais m'entraîner à

- Comprendre ce qui est en train de se passer.
- Répondre à un questionnaire sur les styles vestimentaires.
- Décrire une action en cours, un problème.
- Parler de ce qui est en train de se passer.
- Raconter le déroulement d'une « première ».

Je vais utiliser

Le présent en *be* + *V-ing* .... p. 97

Le lexique des vêtements.

Les verbes d'action.

→ Go to your WB p. 80

Discover

1 a) Listen to the words and repeat them.
b) Then, match the words with the numbers.

a shirt | a jacket | trousers
shoes | a cap | a jumper

2 What kind of star are you? Answer the question and find your style. Then report to the class!

Wordgym → Go to your WB p. 87

City wear (trousers, skirts, jackets...) or sportswear (t-shirt and jeans)?

CITY WEAR
Do you like **jewellery** (necklaces, rings and bracelets)?
Yes ← / No →

Fashionable
Like Beyonce or Justin Timberlake, you're a real star: everybody notices you!

Classy
Like Brad Pitt or Angelina Jolie, you are elegant and simple. Bravo!

SPORTSWEAR
Do you like tracksuits, caps and necklaces?
Yes ← / No →

Sophisticated
Like Avril Lavigne or 50 Cent, you like to shine! You're so cool!

Casual
Like Johnny Depp or Scarlett Johansson, clothes are not important for you. You've got natural class!

3 a) Listen and put the pictures in the right order.

a

b

c

b) Now sing along!

→ Go to your WB p. 87

Listen and speak

CD ÉLÈVE PISTE 14

4 **a) Look at the first picture and react. Listen and make a list of Mrs Monroe's problems.**

b) → Go to your WB p. 88

Tactics

Savoir repérer les verbes au présent en *be* + V-*ing* t'aidera à mieux comprendre l'état d'esprit des personnages.

Words to remember

CD CLASSE

- cheap
- **com**fortable
- a dress
- ex**pen**sive
- **fa**shion
- a pair of **trou**sers
- put on
- a shirt
- tight
- try on

Don't forget!

1. Le présent en *be* + *V-ing*

*What **are** you do**ing**?*

*I'**m** com**ing**!*

*I'**m** not jok**ing**!*

2. La prononciation de « ea »

*r**ea**d ≠ r**ea**dy*

[iː] [e]

→ Go to your WB p. 89

QUICK CHECK → WB p. 92

Use what you know

5 Speak in pairs

a) The actors are not ready and the director is furious!

Pupil A is the director and pupil B is the assistant.

Pupil A: What is... doing?

Pupil B: She / He's...

b) Sing along « Too bad for you »

6 Speak for a minute

Choose a situation and react: you protest or find a good excuse.
Use one verb in *be + V-ing* minimum.

A Mrs Monroe asks you to come at 7 p.m. because there's a lot of work for the show.
You: *Sorry, Miss, but...*

B She says you aren't ready at all for the show.
You: *But, Miss, ...*

→ Go to your WB p. 90

C She thinks you don't work hard enough.
You: ...

D She says you mustn't use your mobile.
You: ...

YOUR TASK

7 Do a live report.

You are reporting before the premiere of a new musical.

1. Look at the characters and say what's happening and what the people are doing!
You: The dancers are... The singers are... The actors are...
2. Say why the director is angry.

→ Go to your WB p. 90

Grammar

■ Le présent en *Be + V-ing*

➜ Tu utilises le présent en ***be + V-ing*** pour **décrire une action en cours au moment où tu parles.**

➜ Le présent en ***be + V-ing*** est composé de l'auxiliaire ***be*** suivi de **la base verbale + *-ing*.**

Forme affirmative	*I'**m** com**ing**.* *She'**s** speak**ing** on the phone.* *We'**re** work**ing**.*
Forme interrogative	*What **are** you do**ing**?* ***Is** he com**ing**?*
Forme négative	*I'**m not** jok**ing**!* *They **are not** work**ing**.*

➜ Le présent en ***be + V-ing*** associé à une certaine intonation de ta voix te permet de **faire un commentaire** sur ce que tu vois.

Oh, no, it's raining again.

➜ ***Be*** + **V-*ing*** te permet de parler d'une action en cours en ajoutant un message supplémentaire (explication, reproche, avertissement, justification...).

Tom: I'm sorry Chad, I can't help you now!
*I'**m doing** my homework...*

(Tom donne comme excuse à Chad qu'il est en train de faire ses devoirs. En français aussi on utilise ce procédé : *Désolé Chad, je ne peux pas t'aider : je suis en train de faire mes devoirs !*)

⚠ come ➞ com**ing** — write ➞ writ**ing**
cut ➞ cut**ting** — stop ➞ stop**ping**

Exercises

1 Complète les phrases suivantes avec *is* ou *are*.

a. No, we... not playing, we... working!
b. What... Scarlett doing?
c. ... you having a good time?
d. Where... he calling from?
e. They... getting ready for the show.

2 Mr Williams téléphone à Mrs Williams. Complète la conversation en mettant les verbes au présent en *be* + V-*ing*.

– Hello, Sylvia!
– Kevin! Where *(you/call)* from?
– I *(call)* from the airport. I *(come)* to London!
– That's fantastic! What a nice surprise! Why *(you/come)*?
– To see Scarlett's show. *(she/work)* at the moment?
– Yes, she *(do)* her homework! Wait, she *(come)*.

3 Relis le script du dialogue p.152 et corrige les phrases ci-dessous.

Ex.: Mrs Monroe is talking to Mrs Clarke.
➞ She isn't speaking to Mrs Clarke, she's speaking to Tom, Chad and Scarlett.

a. Mrs Monroe and the children are preparing an opera.
b. Tom is trying on a coat.
c. Scarlett is speaking to her mother.
d. Scarlett's father is calling from Paris.

More exercises ➜ p. 154 CD ÉLÈVE Audio-Rom

ENGLISH LAB (CD CLASSE) La prononciation de « ea »

1 Écoute les mots suivants et classe-les dans le tableau ci-dessous.
sweat-shirt – meat – ready – meal – eat – read

2 Tu remarques que « ea » peut se prononcer :

[iː]	[e]
comme dans *meat*	comme dans *ready*

3 Lis les phrases suivantes à voix haute.
a. Are you ready to eat?
b. I'm not ready to wear this sweat-shirt.
c. Stop reading and eat your meat.

More exercises ➜ CD ÉLÈVE Audio-Rom

Language practice

Practise your **vocabulary**

1 Retrouve 6 mots désignant des vêtements dans la grille. Écris-les dans ton cahier. Tu peux t'aider des dessins.

F	N	B	A	W	C	S	Y	D	J	S
Z	K	M	K	W	O	V	Y	J	S	E
S	E	O	H	S	A	M	A	E	N	R
X	P	G	K	H	T	C	R	C	A	P
S	P	I	J	B	K	D	M	H	P	P
F	R	F	U	E	Q	P	Y	H	C	P
T	B	Z	T	R	I	H	S	L	R	T

2 Es tu capable de nommer :

a. deux vêtements qui commencent par la lettre « s » ?
b. deux vêtements qui commencent par la lettre « c » ?
c. un vêtement qui commence par la lettre « j » ?
d. un accessoire qui commence par la lettre « n » ?

Practise your **grammar**

3 Réponds aux questions suivantes en fonction de ce qui se passe au moment où tu fais l'exercice.

a. What are you doing?
b. Is it raining?
c. What are your parents doing?
d. Are you dancing?
e. What is your best friend doing?

4 Retrouve les questions qui ont provoqué ces réponses.

a. No, I'm not dancing, I'm working.
b. No, it isn't raining, it's very sunny.
c. No, we are not chatting, Sir, we are listening.
d. No, I'm not crying, I'm acting.
e. No, they aren't speaking on the phone, they're chatting on the internet.

Practise your **pronunciation**

CD CLASSE

5 Écoute et classe les mots suivants en deux colonnes selon la prononciation de « ea ».

eat meat ready
read dead please

HAVE FUN

6 Repeat these tongue twisters.

I scream when I eat ice cream!

Eat your meal: it's veal and cream!

Unit 12

Part 5

A great musical

Je vais m'entraîner à

- Comprendre ce que quelqu'un a dû faire.
- Comprendre l'essentiel de la critique d'un spectacle.
- Décrire un problème et dire ce que l'on a dû faire.
- Interviewer quelqu'un sur ses expériences.
- Réécrire un court article.

Je vais utiliser

Les pronoms personnels compléments ..... p. 103

Had to .... p. 103

Le lexique du spectacle.

Go to your WB p. 80

Discover

1 **a) Listen and repeat the words about show business.** C.D. CLASSE

actor actress singer dancer director

b) Look and speak about their jobs.

You: Miley Cyrus is a famous.../ Charlie Chaplin was...

Miley Cyrus

Charlie Chaplin

Fred Astaire

Keira Knightley

Robert Pattinson

Wordgym → Go to your WB p. 93

2 **Listen to the interview of Julia Simmons, a famous actress. She tells us about her new film "Queen of the Gorillas". What happened to her ?** C.D. CLASSE

→ Go to your WB p. 93

3 **a) Read the article.**
b) Find transparent words.
c) Say who the pronouns "her", "him"and "them" refer to.

Julia Simmons' new film!

An exclusive interview by Michael Morris.

In her new film, "Queen of the Gorillas", Julia Simmons had a hard time: she had to spend three months with three gorillas in a hostile jungle. At first they did not accept her, but after three months, they loved her and she loved them! Julia says that her worst nightmare was to kiss her partner Simon Juliano: she hates him as much as he hates her! And she had to kiss him three times. An actress's life can sometimes be very difficult.

Read and speak

4 **a) Look at the document: what kind of document is it? What is it about?**
b) Do you think the show was a success or not?

→ Go to your WB p. 94

Tactics

- Pour comprendre un texte écrit, appuie-toi sur les éléments connus : les noms des personnages, ce que tu sais d'eux.
- Repère aussi les mots que tu connais déjà et les mots « transparents » (= qui ressemblent au français).

Fame: a great success
Scarlett Williams: a new star?

YESTERDAY'S PERFORMANCE OF "FAME, THE MUSICAL", DIRECTED BY ANGELINA MONROE, WAS A GREAT SUCCESS.

A lot of pupils and parents came to see it. They had to queue for 30 minutes in order to buy the tickets. At the end of the performance, everybody was applauding and shouting "encore!". Scarlett Williams, the main actress, had to sing an extra song to satisfy the audience.
"This was my first acting experience", she told us. "It was very hard work. I had to learn a lot of pages by heart.

Also, we had to exercise a lot because the choreography was very difficult. And I had to dance and sing at the same time! It was hard, but I loved it. Now I know that I want to be an actress". A lot of people in Kingston already admire her!
Unfortunately, Chad O'Malley, alias Steve, forgot the lyrics of his song. His teacher had to come on stage to help him. She had to sing with him.
After the show, Mrs Monroe congratulated her students. She said to them: " This was a great evening for me. I know that it was difficult for you and that you had to make a great effort to be ready on time. But I am very proud of you and I'm counting on you to do « West Side Story » next year".

Liz Simonson and Diane Mellor
The Kingston Gazette

Words to remember

- ap**plaud**
- the **au**dience
- the **ly**rics
- the per**for**mance
- the show
- the stage

Don't forget!

1. Les pronoms personnels compléments
She had to sing with him!
A lot of people admire her.

2. La prononciation de *had to*
I had to learn a lot of pages by heart.

→ Go to your WB p. 95

QUICK CHECK → WB p. 98

Use what you know

5 Write a few lines

You're a journalist. There are too many repetitions in this article! Rewrite it.

You: Troy and Gabriella meet during a holiday → They meet during a holiday.

Troy listening to Sharpay

High School Musical is a love story between Troy and Gabriella. Troy and Gabriella meet during a holiday. Troy sings a karaoke with Gabriella and Troy thinks Gabriella is fantastic. When Troy goes back to school Troy sees Gabriella again. Gabriella is a new pupil. Gabriella meets Troy's friends, Sharpay and Ryan. Sharpay asks Troy "Do you want to be in the show with Ryan and me?". When Sharpay discovers that Gabriella can sing better than Sharpay, Sharpay becomes furious...

→ Go to your WB p. 96

6 Speak for a minute

Mrs Mason had a very busy day. She had to prepare the show. Read her diary and say what she had to do.

You: She had to...

9 AM:	Prepare the costumes for the show
10 AM:	Help Scarlett to learn her choreography
11 AM:	Paint the setting
12 PM:	Repair Chad's costume
1 to 4 PM:	English lessons
5 PM:	Help Chad to learn his song
6 PM:	Prepare the stage

→ Go to your WB p. 96

YOUR TASK

7 Interview a star.

1. Prepare five questions for a star.
2. One pupil in the class is the star. The class asks him/her questions.
3. The "star" must answer the questions without saying any names!

He or she wins after two minutes.

*Ex.: Did you have to kiss **Robert Pattinson**? → Yes, I had to kiss **him**.*

Grammar

Les pronoms personnels compléments

➜ Tu utilises les pronoms personnels compléments **pour ne pas avoir à répéter** le nom de la personne ou de l'objet dont tu parles.

Pronoms personnels sujets	Pronoms personnels compléments
I	me
you	you
he	him
she	her
it	it
we	us
you	you
they	them

*Mrs Monroe congratulated her students. She said to **them**...*

Had to

➜ Tu utilises ***had to*** suivi d'une base verbale pour dire ce que quelqu'un a dû faire.

*I **had to** dance and sing at the same time.*

Forme affirmative	She had to sing another song.

⚠ ***Had to*** remplace ***must*** au passé.

Exercises

1 Complète ces phrases avec le pronom personnel qui convient.

a. I don't know Julia Simmons. Do you know...?
b. We are going to see "Les Misérables". Do you want to come with...?
c. I don't know the actors in this show. Do you know...?
d. Asher Book? Oh, yes, I love ...!
e. "Grease" was on TV last night. Did you watch...?

2 Complète avec *must* ou *had to*.

a. We are late! You... hurry up!
b. It was very difficult. I... learn a lot of pages by heart.
c. Look, it's raining, we... go home now.
d. A dog attacked us: we... run very fast.
e. The audience was calling the actors: Scarlett... sing another song.

3 Retrouve de qui on parle dans chaque phrase. Choisis parmi les deux possibilités.

a. A lot of people admire him. (*Elizabeth II/ Barack Obama*)
b. They gave a lot of concerts last year. (*Britney Spears/ The Jonas Brothers*)
c. Nicole Kidman acted in "Australia" with him. (*Scarlett Johansson/Hugh Jackman*)
d. A lot of girls are afraid of them but they love them! (*Robert Pattison/Vampires*)
e. Johnny Depp loves her! (*Vanessa Paradis/ Johnny Depp's children*)

More exercises ➜ p. 154

CD ÉLÈVE Audio-Rom

ENGLISH LAB CD CLASSE

La prononciation de « had to »

1 Écoute les phrases suivantes.

a. I had to kiss him.
b. They had to work a lot.
c. Did you have to sing in the show?

2 Tu remarques que dans l'expression « had to », « to » n'est pas accentué et se prononce /tə/.

3 Lis les phrases suivantes à voix haute.

a. She had to run and she had to jump.
b. Why did she have to live with three gorillas?
c. I had to dance and sing at the same time.
d. The spectators had to queue for a long time.

More exercises ➜ CD ÉLÈVE Audio-Rom

Language practice

Practise your **vocabulary**

1 Find the words.

a. It is where the actors act.

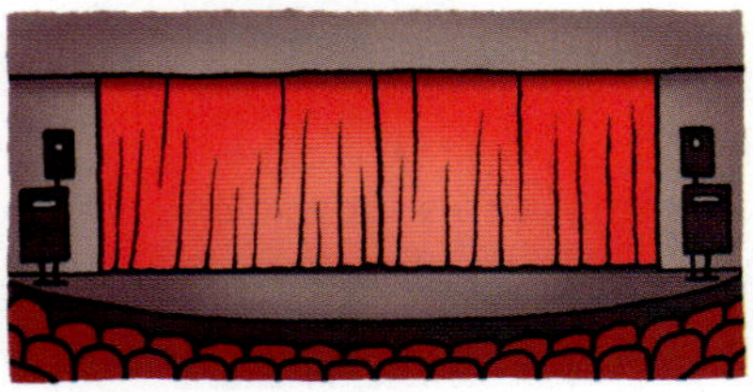

b. They are the people who watch the show.

c. Another word for "show".

d. It is the building where they act.

e. Feminine of "actor".

Practise your **grammar**

2 Relis l'article p. 101 et complète ce résumé avec *had to* et des pronoms personnels.

The show was a great success. The audience called Scarlett. They wanted to see… again! She… come back on stage and sing another song for… Chad did not remember his text. He completely forgot… His teacher … help… She came on stage and sang with… Mrs Monroe was very proud of her pupils: she congratulated…

3 Cathy et Pam, deux filles de l'école, ont vu le spectacle. Complète leur conversation.

Cathy: I loved the show last night! Did you enjoy…?
Pam: Yes, it wasn't bad. But who was that guy? Do you know…?
Cathy: Who, Tom? Yes, of course I know… He was very good. At the beginning, I couldn't recognize…!
Pam: And who was the actress? Do you know…?
Cathy: She's the new girl, she's American. You know, she's always with Tom and Chad, I think she likes…

4 Réponds à ces questions en utilisant un pronom personnel complément.

a. Do you know the Simpsons?
b. Do you like Charlie Chaplin?
c. Do you know Marilyn Monroe?
d. Do you like going to the cinema?

Practise your **pronunciation**

5 Entraîne-toi à répéter ces phrases.

The teacher had to teach them how to dance too.

Julia Simmons had to live with three gorillas.

Check your progress

1 Listen

Which film is better?

ton objectif Comprendre une interview.

Les comparatifs • Les pronoms personnels.

Es-tu capable de :

- A1 1. comprendre le sujet général de l'interview ?
- A1+ 2. dire lequel des deux films est une comédie ?
- A2 3. dire lequel des deux films John Cannon a préféré tourner et pourquoi ?

→ Go to your WB p. 100

2 Read

A message from Mark

ton objectif Comprendre un e-mail.

Had to • Les pronoms personnels.

Lis cet e-mail.

From: markthompson@myworld.co.uk

To: kenbarber@yahoo.co.uk

Dear Ken,
I'm so sorry I could not go to the cinema with you yesterday. Did you wait for me?
It was impossible for me to come or to call you because I got a very bad mark for my maths test. I got an E! My dad was so furious ! He confiscated my phone and my computer. I had to do extra maths exercises all afternoon! I had to copy my lesson out ten times! It was horrible.
See you soon,
Mark

Es-tu capable de :

- A1 1. comprendre dans quel but Mark écrit cet e-mail ?
- A1+ 2. comprendre pourquoi il n'a pas pu faire ce qu'il voulait ?
- A2 3. comprendre ce qu'il a dû faire à la place ?

→ Go to your WB p. 100

3 Speak

What are they doing?

ton objectif Décrire ce qui est en train de se passer.

Le présent en *be* + *V-ing*.

L'élève A ferme les yeux et pose des questions à l'élève B sur ce qu'il voit dans la classe et dehors. L'élève B répond à ses questions.
Es-tu capable de :

- A1 1. expliquer ce qui est en train de se passer ?
- A1+ 2. donner des explications supplémentaires ?
- A2 3. réagir en faisant des commentaires sur ce qui se passe ?

→ Go to your WB p. 101

4 Write

Toni, Sheila and the criminals

ton objectif Réécrire un texte en l'améliorant.

Les pronoms personnels compléments.

Ton ami veut présenter un film sur son blog mais le texte n'est pas très clair.

Tiger

Tiger is the story of Sheila, a secret agent, who must infiltrate a dangerous Chinese organisation. Sheila meets Toni, the boss of the secret organization, and she falls in love with Toni.
Toni discovers that Sheila is a secret agent but he decides to defend Sheila. Toni and Sheila fight against a lot of criminals and finally Toni and Sheila defeat a lot of criminals. Toni and Sheila decide to run away together and to start a new life. In the end Toni and Sheila move to Hawai and Toni marries Sheila.

Es-tu capable de :

- A1 1. recopier le texte sans fautes ?
- A1+ 2. raccourcir le texte et le clarifier en évitant les répétitions ?

→ Go to your WB p. 101

Part 5

Discovery

Welcome to Broadway!

CD CLASSE

Can you dance like Michael Jackson? Can you sing like Madonna? If you have all these qualities, you can be a star on Broadway, the famous New York avenue! It is the place where a lot of musicals are taking place.

My Fair Lady (1956)

This famous musical is about a professor who transforms a poor vulgar flower girl into a very elegant lady!

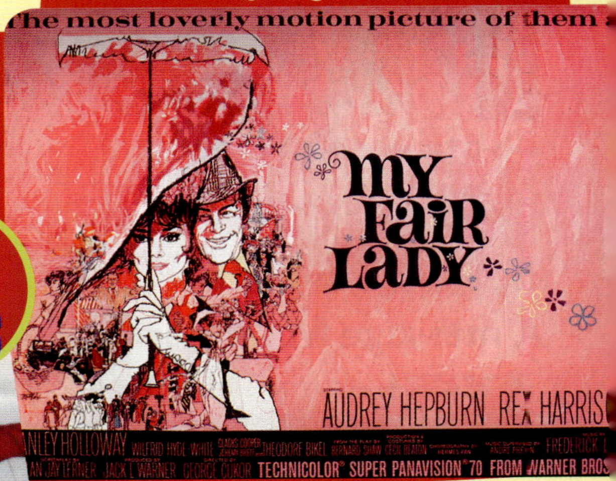

THE 50'S

Singing in the Rain (1952)

It is probably the most famous musical in the world.
It is a film and it is an exception: it was never played on Broadway!

West Side Story

(1957) This Broadway musical became a famous film in 1961. It is a tragic love story based on *Romeo and Juliet*.

The 60's

Hair (1968)

It was played nonstop for four years between 1968 and 1972! It is the musical of the hippie generation.

Grease (1972).
This monument of the disco generation was made into a film in 1978. Thanks to *Grease*, American musicals are very popular everywhere in the world.

The 70's

The 80's

Fame (1980)
It was a TV series then a film, and finally a Broadway musical. The action takes place in an academy of Arts. All the pupils want to become famous.

NOWADAYS...

High School Musical

The theatre version *High School Musical on Stage* is the musical most played in schools in the U.S.A.

Quiz time

Can you name:

1. the boulevard where lots of musicals are created in New York?
2. the musical adaptation of *Romeo and Juliet*?
3. the musical that takes place in an academy of Arts?
4. the names of two musicals that were films before becoming shows?
5. the name of the famous musical that was never played on Broadway?

FINAL TASK

Act out the last scene of *High School Musical*.

1 Read the summary of the last scene.

Mrs Darbus, the English teacher, and Mr Bolton, the sports teacher, are discussing who they are going to choose for the role of their musical: Sharpay or Gabriella.

Mrs Darbus prefers Sharpay but Mr Bolton prefers Gabriella.

Sharpay arrives: she explains why she is better than Gabriella, and what she had to do to prepare for the role.

Gabriella calls Mrs Darbus with her mobile phone.
She explains why she is late: she explains what she had to do.
Gabriella arrives and sings a song: she IS the new star!

2 In groups of four, choose your roles and write the dialogue.

3 Act out the scene in front of the class. The class votes for the best version.

www.broadwaymusicalhome.com

Part 6 Across the sea

Sweet Mary

PISTE 15 Karaoké

In a small and lovely cottage
Lived a girl, her name was Mary
There she was, the fairest maiden
Like a red rose by the sea.
And the high winds tell her story
And the black rocks tell her pain
As she waited for her Cory
Every morning in the rain.

Chorus
Oh Mary, sweet Mary,
We'd like to see your smile
Oh Mary, dear Mary,
We'd like to hear your laugh
You waited for your lost love
Long gone into the sea
You waited for your lost love
Long gone into the sea.

When she met her handsome Cory,
It was a bright and shiny day
He was tall, she was a beauty
When they first met in the bay
What a beauty! What a lady!
What a handsome man he was!
And they bonded[1] for eternity
As they stood facing the sea! (...)

1. Ils se lièrent

Unit 13 Off to Ireland

Je vais m'entraîner à

- Comprendre des informations sur l'organisation d'un voyage.
- Parler des projets de quelqu'un.
- Discuter de ce que l'on aimerait faire. Partager mes sentiments et mes réactions.
- Écrire un e-mail à l'Office de tourisme d'Irlande pour demander des renseignements.

Je vais utiliser

Would like, should........ p. 113

Les phrases exclamatives............... p. 113

Le lexique du voyage et des transports.

→ Go to your WB p. 102

Discover

1 **a) Listen and match the words with the right picture.**

train car plane ferry bicycle bus

1

2

3

4

5

6

b) Look at the map p. II and say what means of transport you can use to go from London to Dublin. Find as many possibilities as you can.

You: You can go from London to Dublin by...

Wordgym → Go to your WB p. 103

2 **Listen to the conversation between Mr and Mrs Clarke and a travel agent. What do they choose for their trip to Ireland?**

You: They...

→ Go to your WB p. 103

3 **Listen and say if the person speaks about what he wants to do in the future or what he did in the past.**

→ Go to your WB p. 103

Listen and speak

PISTE 16

4 a) **Look at the first picture and react. Where are Scarlett, Tom and Chad?**
b) **Imagine who the lady is.**
c) **Now listen to the conversation: say who the old lady is and find information about her life.**

→ Go to your WB p. 104

Tactics

Le contexte et les formes verbales t'aident à repérer si les personnages parlent du passé ou de l'avenir.

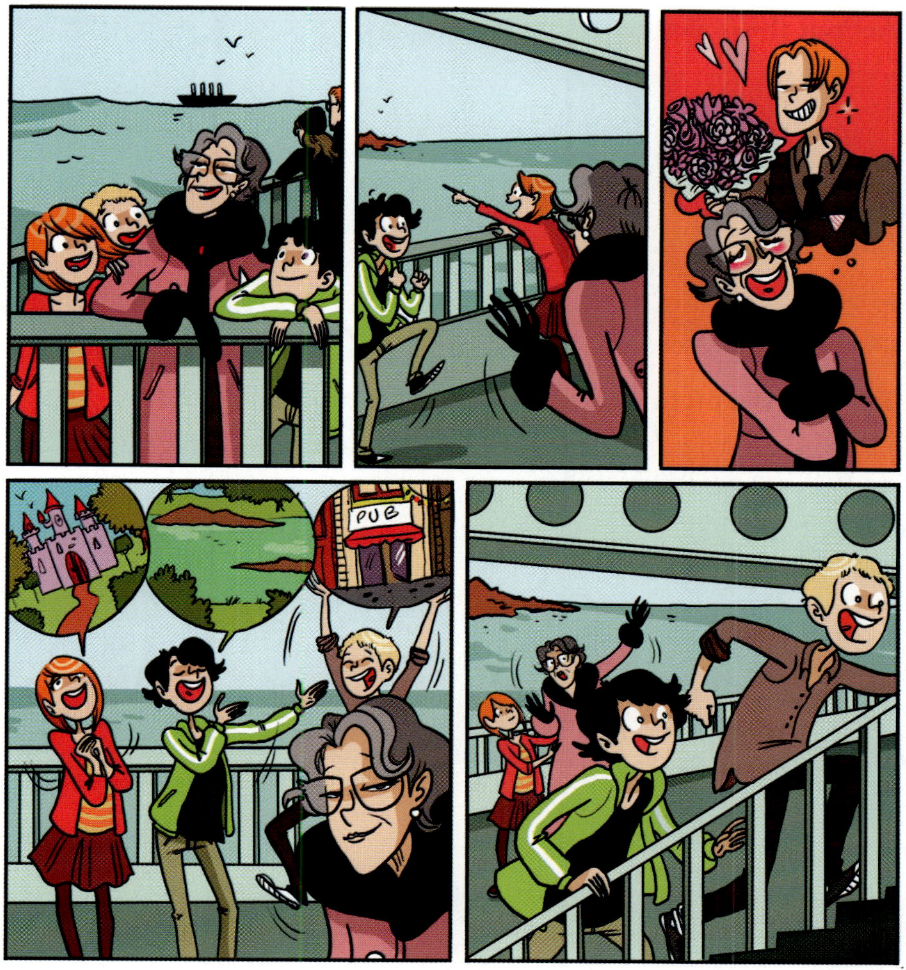

Words to remember

CD CLASSE

- arrive
- coast
- a deck
- a **har**bour
- an **is**land
- a **lake**
- the **land**scape
- leave = go away
- a **pas**senger
- a pub
- **tra**vel

Don't forget!

1. WOULD LIKE
Would you like some tea?

2. SHOULD
You should go to Ireland!

3. Les phrases exclamatives avec *what* et *so*
What a nice story!
It's so charming!

→ Go to your WB p. 105

QUICK CHECK → WB p. 108

Use what you know

5 Speak in pairs

a) Decide:

- where you would like to go in Ireland.
- what you should visit there.

b) Say why.

You: I'd like… I / you / we should… because it's so… !

c) Act out the dialogue.

sports on the lake

typical Irish shops

going for a walk on the moors

d) React to the pictures and say where you would like to stay.

Pupil A: I'd like to… / I wouldn't like to… because the cottage is / it's so…
Pupil B: What a… I'd like…

a caravan

a bed and breakfast

a five star hotel

→ Go to your WB p. 106

YOUR TASK

6 Write an email to the Tourism Board of Ireland to ask for some information.

1. Explain how you would like to travel.
2. Say where you would like to stay.
3. Explain what you would like to visit.
4. Mention when you would like to travel.
5. Ask for prices.

→ Go to your WB p. 106

Video Flash DVD

Book a ticket for Ireland

Grammar

■ Would like

➜ Tu utilises ***would like*** **+ nom ou pronom** pour dire ce que tu aimerais, ce que tu voudrais.
Tu utilises ***would like to*** **+ base verbale** pour dire ce que tu aimerais faire.

Forme affirmative	Forme interrogative	Forme négative
*I'**d like** to stay in a cottage.*	***Would** you **like** to stay in a cottage?*	*I **wouldn't like** to stay in a cottage.*

⚠ ***'d*** est la contraction de ***would***.
Would est un auxiliaire de modalité. Il se place entre le sujet et le verbe.

■ Should

➜ Tu utilises ***should*** pour **donner un conseil ou faire une recommandation**, donc dire à quelqu'un **ce qu'il devrait faire ou ne devrait pas faire**.

Forme affirmative	Forme négative
Sujet + ***should*** + base verbale *You should listen to me!* *We should visit Bunratty Castle.*	***should not*** = ***shouldn't*** *You shouldn't listen to Chad!*

■ Les phrases exclamatives

Tu utilises ***so*** ou ***what*** pour former des phrases exclamatives.

➜ ***So*** + adjectif !

*This story is **so** beautiful !*
*These flowers are **so** nice!*

➜ ***What a*** + nom singulier ! et ***What*** + nom pluriel !

***What a** nice story!*
***What** nice flowers!*

Exercises

1 La classe organise un voyage en Irlande. Explique ce que les élèves aimeraient faire.

a. **Mary:** go to a concert in Dublin.
b. **Jack, Tom, Matthew:** see a rugby match.
c. **Lucy, Anne:** visit haunted castles.
d. **Mark:** do kite surfing in the Aran Islands.
e. **Scott, Albert and Andrew:** go on a tour in a horse-drawn caravan.

2 Utilise chaque couple de mots pour écrire deux exclamations : l'une avec *what* et l'autre avec *so*.

Ex.: lucky/boy ➞ What a lucky boy!
This boy is so lucky!

a. big/castle
b. beautiful/lakes
c. interesting/story
d. fast/ship
e. fascinating/country

3 Traduis en anglais.

a. J'aimerais visiter le château de Bunratty.
b. J'aimerais faire du bateau dans la mer d'Irlande.
c. Tu devrais faire tes devoirs.
d. Elle aimerait voyager dans une roulotte à cheval.
e. Vous devriez aller à Glendalough.

More exercises ➜ p. 154 CD Élève Audio-Rom

ENGLISH LAB — L'intonation des phrases exclamatives

CD Classe

1 Écoute les phrases suivantes.

a. What a funny lady!
b. This ship is so big!
c. What a beautiful country!
d. This boy is so funny!

2 Que remarques-tu sur l'intonation des exclamations ? Est-elle montante ou descendante ?

3 Écoute les phrases et dis si ce sont des questions ou des exclamations.

More exercises ➜ CD Élève Audio-Rom

Language practice

Practise your **vocabulary**

1 Remet les lettres dans l'ordre et retrouve 5 moyens de transport. Fais correspondre les mots avec les dessins.

a. ryref b. nepal c. nitar d. toba e. sbu

1

2

3

4

5

2 Complète avec le moyen de transport qui convient.

a. You cannot go from Great Britain to Ireland by...
b. The fastest way to go from London to Dublin is by...
c. It's nice to cross the Irish Sea on a...
d. Do you take the... to go to school every morning?
e. It's nice to use a... during the summer.

HAVE FUN (CD CLASSE)

Listen and sing along
Old Sam Daniels

Practise your **grammar**

3 Relis le script du dialogue p. 152 et remet les phrases dans le bon ordre.

a. tea / like / with / Rose / would / sandwiches / and / cucumber / some
b. Scarlett / know / to / like / about / would / love / Rose's / first
c. Rose / Chad / listen / thinks / should / story / her / too / to

4 Écris les exclamations que tu utiliserais dans les situations suivantes.

a. Tu es devant un énorme navire.
b. Tu vois une toute petite maison.
c. Tu découvres un merveilleux paysage.
d. Tu entends une histoire incroyable.
e. Un ami te donne une excellente idée.

Practise your **pronunciation** (CD CLASSE)

5 Lis les énoncés suivants avec la bonne intonation. Écoute pour vérifier ta prononciation.

a. What? A man?
b. What a man!
c. What? An old lady?
d. What an old lady!

6 Entraîne-toi à lire ces exclamations en accentuant « *so* ».

a. This story is so incredible!
b. Rose is so old!
c. Chad is so lucky to go to Ireland!
d. This country is so nice!

Unit 14 The magic island

Je vais m'entraîner à

- Comprendre des éléments de chronologie.
- Comprendre un court récit au passé.
- Raconter des événements passés. Situer des événements dans le passé.
- Poser des questions sur des célébrités irlandaises ou l'histoire de l'Irlande et y répondre.
- Compléter un axe du temps.

Je vais utiliser

Les questions au prétérit........ p. 119

Le prétérit avec *ago*........... p. 119

Le lexique de la nature et des paysages.

→ Go to your WB p. 102

Discover

1 Listen and match the words with the right numbers.

castle | village | lake
harbour | forest | town
sea | beach | hill
river | road

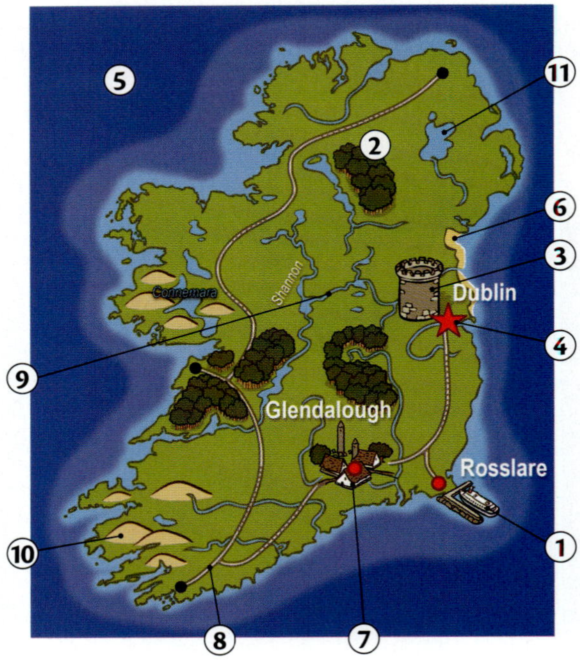

Wordgym → Go to your WB p. 109

2 Ireland has magic inhabitants! Read this legend.

a) What happened to the boy?

b) What choice did he make? What is the moral of the story?

Leprechauns are little green elves[1] who live in Ireland. They make shoes and they are very rich. They can bring good luck or bad luck. They live in the forest, at the end of the rainbow. One day, a long, long time ago, a young boy found a leprechaun. The leprechaun said to him “If you promise to let me go, I will show you where my treasure is”. The boy accepted. The leprechaun took the boy to a cave[2] near the sea. In the cave, there was a cauldron[3] full of gold. The boy only took two gold coins. He didn't take the cauldron. With the money, the boy bought books. He went to university and became a very good student. After, he made a lot of money. The story shows that studies are more important than a cauldron of gold!

1. elfes **2.** grotte **3.** chaudron

→ Go to your WB p. 109

3 Listen and match the years in your workbook.

around 1915 — around 1935 — around 1940 — the day before yesterday

→ Go to your WB p. 109

Listen and speak

CD ÉLÈVE PISTE 17

4 a) Look at the second picture and guess who the old man is.

b) Imagine what Rose and he are talking about.

c) Find information about the man's life.

→ Go to your WB p. 110

Tactics

Apprends à repérer *ago* et les unités de temps (*day, year*, etc.) : ils t'aideront à situer les événements dans le temps et à mieux comprendre un récit.

Words to remember

CD CLASSE

- **ago**
- be born
- **cen**tury
- disap**pear**
- leave
- month
- old
- year
- young

Don't forget!

1. Les questions au prétérit

Why did you disappear?
Where did you go?

2. La prononciation de « o »

ago	*come*	*not*
/əʊ/	/ʌ/	/ɒ/

→ Go to your WB p. 111

QUICK CHECK → WB p. 114

Use what you know

5 Speak in pairs

Choose one of these three Irish men.
The class asks questions and guesses who it is.

The class: When was he born? How did he...
You: He was born in...

	Pierce Brosnan	Jonathan Rhys Meyers	Bono
Date of birth	May 16th 1963	July 27th 1977	May 10th 1960
Place of birth	Navan	Dublin	Dublin
Started his career in	New York 1980	London 2000	Was the leader of the band "U2"
Reasons for celebrity	James Bond (2000)	Henry VIII (2007)	His song "Sunday Bloody Sunday" (1983)

→ Go to your WB p. 112

YOUR TASK

6 Quiz your friends about Irish history.

1. Read the important dates of Irish history.
2. Then, quiz your friends. Pupil A chooses a date. Pupil B finds the corresponding question.

Pupil A: The answer is "In 600 BC".
Pupil B: "The question is "When did the Celts invade Ireland"?

→ Go to your WB p. 112

600 BC
The Celts invaded England.

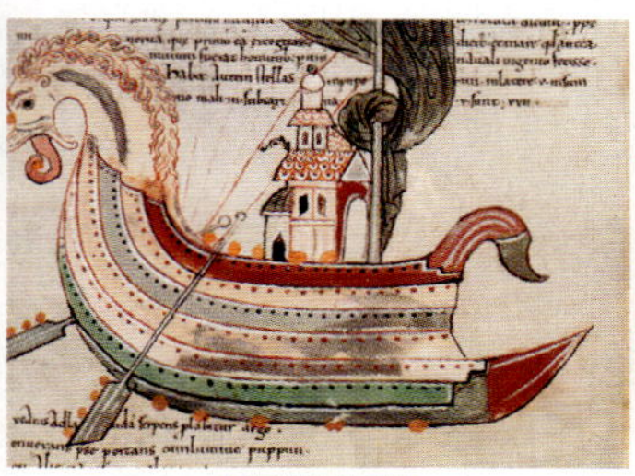

920
The Vikings attacked Ireland.

1169
The Normans invaded Ireland.

1541
King Henry VIII of England became "King of Ireland". Ireland became English.

1921
Ireland became independent.

Grammar

Le prétérit (2)

→ Tu utilises la forme interrogative du prétérit pour **poser des questions au passé.**

__Did__ you __go__ to the USA?

→ Tu utilises les mots en **wh-** (*what, when, who, where, how, why*) placés devant l'auxiliaire ***did*** pour poser une **wh-question** au passé.

__Why__ did you go to the USA? – __When__ did he leave?
__Where__ did you go? – __What__ did he find?

⚠ Lorsque l'auxiliaire est ***be*** la question au prétérit est formulée avec ***was*** ou ***were***.

Where __were__ you born?
When __was__ he born?

Ago

→ Tu utilises **ago** après l'expression de la durée pour indiquer la durée entre un événement passé et le moment présent.

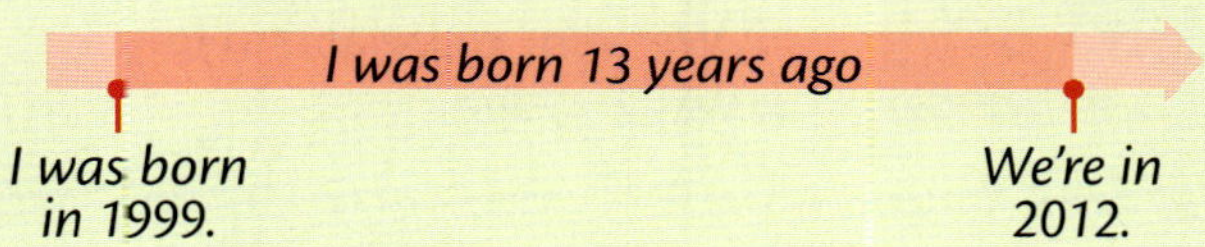

He went to the U.S.A. fifty years __ago__.
The Vikings invaded Ireland six centuries __ago__.

⚠ **Ago** est toujours associé à une unité de temps : *second, minute, hour, day, week, month, year, century* ou "*a long time*".

Exercises

1 Retrouve les *wh- questions* qui ont provoqué les réponses suivantes.

a. He discovered America in 1492.
b. The Vikings invaded England 11 centuries ago.
c. Rose was born 83 years ago.
d. He left Ireland because life was hard.
e. She went to Ireland by boat.

2 Tu souhaites obtenir plus de précisions sur les moments importants de la vie de Danny. Pose un maximum de *wh- questions*.

a. He went to the U.S.A.
b. He found the golden caldron.
c. He met Rose.
d. He studied.

3 Reformule ces phrases en utilisant « *ago* ».

Ex.: *Christopher Columbus discovered America in the 15th century. → Christopher Columbus discovered America 6 centuries ago.*

a. She was born in 1920.
b. He called me at 7 o'clock this morning.
c. I arrived on Monday.
d. She first met John in 1990.
e. I went to New York in 2007.

More exercises → p. 154 CD Élève Audio-Rom

ENGLISH LAB – La prononciation de « o »

CD Classe

1 Écoute et classe les mots que tu entends dans le tableau.

a. go b. love c. Tom

Tu remarques que la lettre "o" peut se prononcer de trois façons différentes.

/əʊ/		/ʌ/	/ɒ/
gold	Rose	come	forest
old	ago	worry	not

2 Entraîne-toi à répéter les phrases suivantes.

a. He found the gold cauldron ten months ago.
b. Come on, go and collect gold!
c. Now, where did you go two days ago?
d. Tom's in the forest with Rose and her love.

More exercises → CD Élève Audio-Rom

Language practice

Practise your **vocabulary**

1 Retrouve la lettre qui manque dans chaque série et tu découvriras des mots décrivant le paysage.

a. H I _ _ V I _ _ A G E C _ I F F

b. S E _ L _ K E B E _ C H

c. F O _ E S T H A _ B O U _ _ O A D

2 Complète les phrases suivantes avec l'élément de paysage qui convient.

a. Leprechauns live at the end of the …

b. Loch Ness is a famous Scottish …

c. Snow White was lost in the …

d. In Moher there are some very high …

e. Rosslare is a famous Irish …

3 Complète avec les mots suivants : *day, month, year, century*

a. Monday is the first … of the week

b. Kylemore Abbey was built in the 16th …

c. 1921 is the … when Ireland became independant.

d. We went to Ireland in July. It was 2 … ago.

Practise your **grammar**

4 Donne l'équivalent en année ou en date des expressions suivantes.

a. two days ago

b. three months ago

c. ten years ago

d. two centuries ago

e. twelve hours ago

5 Traduis en anglais.

a. Pourquoi es-tu parti ?

b. Quand êtes-vous arrivés ?

c. Où a-t-il trouvé les pièces d'or ?

d. Qui a-t-elle rencontré ?

e. Comment êtes vous allés en Irlande ?

Practise your **pronunciation**

CD CLASSE

6 Classe les mots suivants trois par trois selon la prononciation de « o ».

gold forest come

ago old love

Tom worry cross

HAVE FUN

7 Écoute et répète pour t'entraîner à prononcer la phrase suivante.

Tom and Rose found gold near a rainbow two days ago.

Check your progress

1 Listen

Tea time

ton objectif Comprendre ce que quelqu'un a commandé.
Would like.

Mr et Mrs Clarke sont à la cafétéria du ferry qui les ramène d'Irlande.

Coffee	£ 1	1.50 €
Ceylon Tea	£ 1.80	2 €
Irish tea	£ 1.80	2 €
Darjeeling Tea	£ 1.80	2 €
Carrot cake	£ 1.80	2 €
Apple pie	£ 2.20	2.50 €
Tuna sandwiches	£ 1.80	2 €
Cucumber sandwiches	£ 1.80	2 €

Es-tu capable de :

A1 1. repérer les plats mentionnés ?
A1+ 2. prendre leur commande exacte ?
A2 3. expliquer les choix de Mrs Clarke ?

→ Go to your WB p. 116

2 Speak

He lived eight centuries ago...

ton objectif Présenter la vie de personnages du passé.
Ago, what et *so*.

Tu es le guide d'un château hanté.
Tu présentes les fantômes aux touristes.

	Ghost 1 O'Malone	Ghost 2 The green knight	Ghost 3 Patrick Kirk	Ghost 4 Molly Avoy
Date of birth	1200	1850	1650	1350
Date of death	1239	1920	1710	1440
Personality	funny and polite	bad and cruel	strange and tired	romantic and stupid

Es-tu capable de :

A1 1. donner quelques dates de naissance et de mort ?
A1+ 2. décrire la personnalité de chaque fantôme en utilisant des exclamations et *ago* ?

→ Go to your WB p. 116

3 Speak

A musical family

ton objectif Interroger quelqu'un sur des dates.
Les *wh- questions* au prétérit.

Tu es le président du fan club du groupe « The Corrs ». Interroge les nouveaux fans pour tester leurs connaissances !

Dates of birth	Awards	Extra information
Jim: 1964 Sharon: 1970 Caroline: 1973 Andrea: 1974	1999: Brit Awards (best international group) 1999: World Music Awards (best Irish group) 2001: NRJ Music Awards (best international group)	Caroline was "Ireland's most beautiful woman" in 2005. Caroline was born on Saint Patrick's day (March 17th). Mr and Mrs Corr taught the piano to their four children.

Es-tu capable de :

A1 1. poser des questions sur les dates de naissance ?
A2 2. poser des questions précises pour obtenir des informations complémentaires ?

→ Go to your WB p. 117

4 Write

What a horrible place!

ton objectif Décrire une expérience désagréable.
Les phrases exclamatives. *Would like.*

Tu es logé dans une vieille abbaye ! La chambre est sale, tu as peur, tu as froid et tu aimerais rentrer chez toi. Raconte-le à un ami.

Es-tu capable de :

A1 1. exposer ton problème ?
A1+ 2. t'exclamer et dire ce que tu aimerais faire ?
A2 3. donner des détails pour rendre ton récit plus convaincant ?

→ Go to your WB p. 117

Discovery

Magic Ireland!

The Giant's causeway
a fantastic bridge

The Giant's causeway was created by a volcanic eruption 60 million years ago.
The legend says that a giant made it! It is composed of 48,000 stone columns. The landscape is so strange and original!

Kylemore Abbey
a scary school

This mysterious abbey, near the lakes of Connemara, is a boarding-school for girls! They say that during the night, elves and fairies dance on the lake. They say that there are ghosts in the dormitories! What a lovely castle! What a scary school!

Glendalough

It is probably the oldest Celtic village in Ireland. It is full of old stones and Viking ruins. What a fascinating place! Can you find the meaning of Glendalough, and discover the secrets of the old Viking tower?

Did you know?

- Celtic → English
- Glen = valley
- Da = two
- Lough = lake

Dublin

And of course I'd like to show you Dublin, our capital city. Here's the university. It's so nice during the summer! I'd like to study there!
And that's the Rugby Stadium. When Ireland wins a Rugby match, the atmosphere's really magic!

Quiz time

Can you give:

1. the name of the capital of Ireland?
2. the colours of the Irish flag?
3. the name of Ireland's national sport?
4. the name of the place created by a volcanic eruption?
5. the name of the first inhabitants of Ireland?
6. the name of a region famous for its lakes?

FINAL TASK

Organize your ideal tour of Ireland.

1. In groups of three, decide how you would like to travel (by plane, car, boat…) and where you would like to sleep (in a hotel, a bed and breakfast…).
2. Describe the places and monuments you'd like to visit. Do not forget to give some historical information!
3. Say which Irish celebrity you'd like to meet during the trip. Give some information about his/her life.
4. Present your work to the class and try to convince them!

www.discoverireland.com

Part 7 Challenges

Join the team!

CD ÉLÈVE PISTE 18 Karaoké

1) The players are ready for tonight
The players are ready for the fight!
And we'll be the best for the fight tonight!
And we're gonna win the match tonight

Chorus

Coz' we're the best, we're the fastest;
We're the strongest; we're the brightest!
We're the champions; we're the kings
You can cheer! And you can sing!
We're the best, we're the team
All together you can scream
We're the champions of the dream
You can cheer[1]! And you can scream:
"Join the Team! Join the Team!"

2) And great players do not know defeat!
And great players never never cheat[2]!
And we'll be the best for the fight tonight!
And we're gonna win the match tonight!

1. applaudir 2. tricher

Unit 15 Who's going to win?

Je vais m'entraîner à

- Comprendre les intentions de quelqu'un.
- Comprendre un court poème.
- Parler de mes projets pour des vacances.
- Discuter du programme d'un week-end.
- Écrire le programme d'un séjour en camp de sport.

Je vais utiliser

Be going to........ p. 129

Les comparatifs (2)

Le lexique du sport (1)

Les verbes d'action liés au sport.

→ Go to your WB p. 118

Discover

1 **How many sports do you know?**

a) Listen and match sports and the following pictures.

b) Now, match the pictures with the actions.

swim | run | dance | ski | score a try | ice skate | score a goal | ride | cycle | shoot an arrow

Wordgym → Go to your WB p. 119

2 **a) Read the poem and speak about Paul's day.**

Today's going to be a good day.
Look at the sun! It's not going to rain.
I've got a ball and we're going to play
After the match we're going to sing "hurray"
Oh yes I'm sure! Today's going to be a good day!

b) Now imagine a bad day and report to the class. → Go to your WB p. 119

3 **Listen and match voices and personalities.**

Listen and speak

CD ÉLÈVE PISTE 19

4 **a) Look at the first picture. Speak about Tom's feelings and intentions.**

b) → Go to your WB p. 120

Tactics

Fais attention au ton des personnages. Après avoir repéré qui parle, concentre-toi sur le ton qu'il prend et sur la façon dont il insiste sur certains mots afin de deviner sa personnalité.

Words to remember

CD CLASSE

- beat
- a defeat
- fall
- lose
- pass
- run
- a team
- win

Don't forget!

1. BE GOING TO

We're going to beat you!
He's going to fall over.
You are not going to win.

2. La prononciation de « ea » (2)

team – defeat /iː/
hear – dear /ɪə/

→ Go to your WB p. 121

QUICK CHECK → WB p. 124

Use what you know

5 Speak for a minute

You're going to Florida on holiday. Speak about your plans.

You: First I ..., then ... and finally...

6 Speak in pairs

a) Ask your friend questions about his plans for the weekend.

Pupil A: What ... on Saturday?
Pupil B: On Saturday, I ...

b) Then report to the class.

→ Go to your WB p. 122

YOUR TASK

7 Plan a sports camp for your class.

1. Think about the destination, accommodation (hotel, house, flat, tent...), duration (a week, a month...).
2. Imagine 5 things you plan to do.
3. Imagine 5 things you are not going to do.
4. Be original: your project can be very strict or totally crazy.

→ Go to your WB p. 122

Grammar

■ Be going to

→ Tu utilises ***be going to*** pour dire ce que tu as **l'intention de faire**.
*I **am going to** run 10 miles.*

→ Tu peux également utiliser ***be going to*** pour prédire ce qui va **se passer** à partir **d'indices dans la situation présente**.
*He's got a tennis racket. He**'s going to** play tennis.*

Forme affirmative	*I**'m going to** win!* *You**'re going to** play the match.*
Forme interrogative	***Am** I **going to** win?* ***Are** you **going to** play the match?*
Forme négative	*I**'m not going to** win.* *You**'re not going to** play the match.*

→ Mémorise : ***be*** conjugué au présent + ***going to*** + **base verbale**

⚠ Seul ***be*** se conjugue !
N'oublie pas de mettre la **base verbale après *to***.

■ Les comparatifs (2)

→ Tu as déjà appris dans *Part* 5 que le comparatif de supériorité se forme différemment selon l'adjectif :
Adjectifs courts → tu ajoutes la terminaison **–er** à l'adjectif.
*I'm strong**er** than you.*
Adjectifs longs → tu utilises **more** devant l'adjectif.
*You're **more** intelligent than Steve.*

→ Il existe des adjectifs qui ne respectent pas cette règle.
Tu devras apprendre leur forme par cœur.
good → **better** bad → **worse**

Exercises

1 Remets les mots dans l'ordre.

a. isn't/Scarlett/to/Steve/support/going/.
b. Tom/score/going/a/is/to/goal/.
c. you/run/before/are/to/going/match/the/?
d. I/to/going/lose/Chad/match/the/think/is/.
e. the/going/throw/am/not/to/to/Tom/I/ball/.

2 À partir des indices donnés, imagine ce qui va se produire.

a. The clouds are black (*rain*).
b. I'm late (*miss the match*).
c. She isn't tired at all (*sleep*).
d. We are ready (*win*).
e. They are well-prepared (*lose*).

3 Complète les phrases avec un comparatif de supériorité.

a. Steve is (*tall*) than Tom but Tom is (*fast*).
b. Scarlett is (*good*) at maths than Chad but Chad is (*good*) at IT.
c. Tom is (*smart*) than Steve.
d. Steve is (*pretentious*) than Chad.

More exercises → p. 154 CD élève Audio-Rom

English Lab — La prononciation de « ea » (2)

CD classe

1 Écoute les mots et classe-les dans le tableau selon le son que tu entends.

/iː/	/ɪə/
team	clear

2 Entraîne-toi! Lis ces phrases à haute voix, puis écoute et vérifie ta prononciation.

a. It's very clear! My team is going to defeat them easily.
b. They can't hear you my dear! Please stop screaming! You're hurting my ears!
c. Dean isn't going to beat Jean.

More exercises → CD élève Audio-Rom

Language practice

Practise your vocabulary

1 Lis ce rébus à haute voix.

2 Trouve l'intrus dans chacune des séries de mots suivants.

a. **Football:** score – goal – swim – ball
b. **Archery:** ball – archer – arrow – bow
c. **Hockey:** goal – skate – dance – score
d. **Basketball:** ride – dribble – basket – run
e. **Rugby:** tackle – kick – dance – score

3 Trouve la définition des mots suivants.

a. A runner is someone who…
b. A swimmer…
c. A player…
d. A rider…
e. A dancer…

Practise your grammar

4 Forme des phrases afin de parler des projets de chacun.

a. **Wendy:** buy a new dress
b. **Dan:** do his homework
c. **Zoe and Tom:** tidy up their bedroom
d. **Me:** learn my lesson
e. **Your maths teacher:** correct the tests

5 Regarde ces dessins et imagine ce qui va se produire.

Practise your pronunciation

HAVE FUN

6 Listen and repeat this sentence.
I didn't hear the name of the dream team clearly, my dear Jean.

Unit 16 A champion team!

Je vais m'entraîner à

- Comprendre des prédictions.
- Comprendre l'essentiel d'un court article de presse.
- Faire des promesses pour obtenir quelque chose.
- Interroger une voyante sur son avenir.
- Imaginer sa vie en 2025 et la raconter.

Je vais utiliser

Will et les marqueurs du futur............p. 133

Le lexique du sport (2).

→ Go to your WB p. 118

Discover

1 **At the stadium: who and what do you see?** CD CLASSE

a) **Listen to the words and repeat them.**

b) **Now match the numbers and the words on the picture.**

the audience · a coach · the fans · the goal · a pitch · players

a referee · the scoreboard · a stadium · a team · whistle

Wordgym → Go to your WB p. 125

2 **Listen and concentrate on the fortune-teller. What are her predictions?** CD CLASSE

→ Go to your WB p. 125

3 **Look at the documents for 30 seconds.**
Then close your book and say what they are. Justify your answer.

Stadium Sports Bar & Grill

BBQ Chicken	£ 3.10
Hot Dog	£ 2.50
Baked potatoe	£ 2.10
Onion soup	£ 1.90

The Bath Chronicle

Monday, June 15th

Bath Rugby Team
wins at home

Football

Football is amazing.
It can also be surprising.
Unlike some other sports
It doesn't matter if you're short

Anyone can play it.
But most people don't show it.
You feel you've had fun.
The moment you have won.

People say it's hard.
But just don't get a yellow card.
Don't worry you'll be fine.
Unless you've committed a crime.

Lorenzo Cilla (11)

Read and speak

4 **a) Look at the document and guess what it is about.**

You: I think it's... because...

b) → Go to your WB p. 126

Tactics

Observe bien la mise en page du document. De quel type de document s'agit-il ? À partir des titres que peux-tu déduire ?

Teddington Youth News

Qualification for Teddington! Congratulations!

Tom Spencer
A new champion

Tom Spencer is our new rugby champion. Last Saturday his team defeated Cambridge Secondary 46 – 3.Tom holds the record[1] with 32 points. Tom's N° 1 fan, Scarlett Williams, declared to our journalist: "Tom is our hero! He's the best player! He's the fastest and the smartest!".

The final

After this amazing game at Kingston, the two teams for the super final will be Teddington versus Oxford. They will meet in London next month, on September 30th and it will be the last tournament[2] of the season.
Tom is really confident about this next match. He told us "We'll work hard for this competition. It's just a question of concentration and team spirit! We won't disappoint[3] you! We'll start training tomorrow morning!". Fingers crossed[4] that this team will continue to make us dream!

Bill Halley
June 30th, 2010

For more information, visit our website **www.teddington.richmond.sch.uk**

1. détient le record 2. tournoi
3. décevoir 4. pourvu que

Words to remember (CD CLASSE)

- a compe**ti**tion
- **con**fident
- congratu**la**tions
- a fan
- hold a **re**cord
- re**cord**
- score
- team **spi**rit
- a **tour**nament
- **train**ing

Don't forget!

1. WILL

It will be the last tournament of the season.
We'll work hard for this competition.
We won't disappoint you.

2. L'accent tonique et le suffixe « -ion »

competition
celebration
congratulations

→ Go to your WB p. 127

QUICK CHECK → WB p. 130

Use what you know

5 Speak for a minute

You want to go to a party with some friends. Convince your parents!

You: I promise I…
Use: lesson / homework / quiet in class / little sister

6 Write a few lines

Imagine your life in 2025. Describe your future house, job, family, hobbies… Be very ambitious!

You: In 2025, I…

Go to your WB p. 128

YOUR TASK

7 Pairwork: play the fortune-telling game.

1. Pupil A (the fortune-teller) imagine 4 predictions about your classmate's future (job, family, money, friends, etc.).
2. Pupil B asks the fortune-teller details about your future life (dates and places).
3. Report to the class.

Go to your WB p. 128

Grammar

■ Will

➜ Tu utilises l'auxiliaire modal ***will*** pour parler du futur.

➜ **Forme affirmative** ➝ *Scarlett **will** go to New York.*
Forme négative ➝ *Tom **will not** play tennis.*
Forme interrogative ➝ ***Will** you go to New York?*

➜ À l'oral, à la forme affirmative, ***will*** se contracte en « ***'ll*** ».
À la forme négative, ***will not*** se contracte en ***won't***.
Will est accompagné d'une **base verbale** (un verbe non conjugué), sauf dans les réponses courtes.
À la forme interrogative, le sujet se place entre ***will*** et la base verbale.
__Will__ you __play__ cricket? Yes, I __will__. No, I __won't__.

➜ Repère les marqueurs du futur.

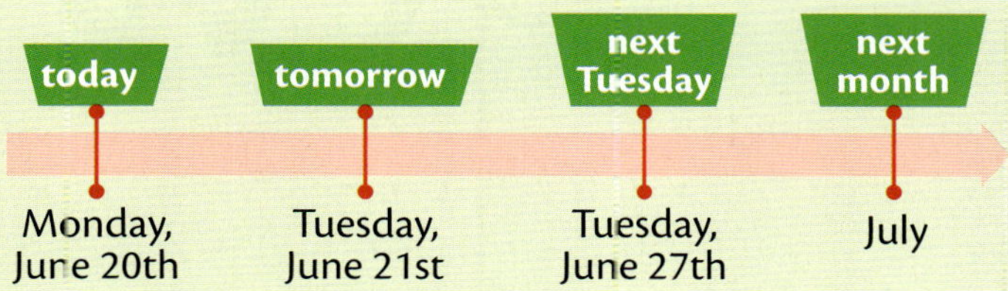

■ Le superlatif de supériorité

➜ Tu utilises un superlatif pour différencier un élément d'un groupe en montrant une caractéristique unique ou exceptionnelle.
*He's **the** smartest!*

➜ **Adjectif court** *the* + adj + *est* *Tom is the fastest.*
Adjectif long *the* + most + *adj* *Steve is the most pretentious.*

➜ **Adjectif irrégulier** *good* ➝ *the best* *bad* ➝ *the worst*

Exercises

1 Lis ces phrases et repère si l'événement est présent, passé ou futur.

a. You'll be a famous singer!
b. He isn't here. He's playing football.
c. They won't support this team next year.
d. Who won the final last year?
e. Will Chelsea defeat Manchester United tomorrow?

2 Reconstitue les prases pour dire ce qui va se passer dans le futur.

a. Chad / play cricket / next year
b. Scarlett / cheer on Tom / next month/ ?
c. Steve / win the school cup
d. Chad and Tom / be friends/ next year
e. You / join the team / ?

3 Construis des superlatifs.

Ex.: Chad runs fast ➝ Chad is the fastest.
a. Tom is smart.
b. Scarlett is beautiful.
c. Chad is funny.
d. Steve is pretentious.
e. Messi is a good player.

More exercises ➜ p. 154 CD ÉLÈVE Audio-Rom

ENGLISH LAB — L'accent tonique et le suffixe « *-ion* »

CD CLASSE

1 Observe, puis écoute ces mots. Tu remarques que l'accent tonique se trouve sur la syllabe qui précède le suffixe « *–ion* ».

champions – congratulations – attention – resolutions

2 Entraîne-toi. Écoute ce poème et amuse-toi à le répéter. Fais attention à la place de l'accent tonique !

Congratulations for your resolutions.
You've got the solutions.
You've got a new mission.
In my opinion you'll become a champion!

More exercises ➜ CD ÉLÈVE Audio-Rom

Language practice

Practise your vocabulary

1 Remets les lettres dans l'ordre sur ton cahier, puis déchiffre le message codé en t'aidant des chiffres.

REEFERE		12	13							
HOACC		8	14		11					
RNTAI				4	5					
MATE	1	2								
HCPIT		9	7							
GOOTALPS	6			10						
SERROCDAOB										3
PERSORUPST							1			

1	2	3	3	4	5	6	1	8	5

W	9	10	10

W	9	5

1	11	12

13	4	5	14	10

Practise your grammar

2 Conjugue correctement le verbe.

a. Tomorrow I (play) football with my friends.
b. You (come) and see me next week?
c. She (watch) the match next Sunday but she (record) it.
d. They are the best and they (win) the next match.
e. We (support) that team but we (support) Chelsea.

3 Montre que tu n'es pas d'accord avec ces affirmations et corrige-les.

a. You will live in a small flat in 2030.
b. You won't have friends next year.
c. Your parents won't give you pocket money next month.
d. You will forget your English copybook in the classroom on Tuesday.
e. Your teachers will be very strict tomorrow.

4 Réponds aux questions suivantes sur ton avenir.

a. Where will you live in 2030?
b. Who will you marry?
c. What will you do for a living? (doctor, reporter, singer, actress…)
d. What car will you drive?
e. How many children will you have?

Practise your pronunciation

CD CLASSE

HAVE FUN

5 Listen to this "chant" and say it.

Congratulations!
You've won the competition!
You've got the selection!
Stand up for the champions!
Let's start the celebrations!

Part 7 Check your progress

1 Listen
Before the match

ton objectif Comprendre une conversation sur un match.

Be going to. Les comparatifs.

Es-tu capable de :

A1
1. dire qui parle ?

A1+
2. dire de quel sport ils / elles parlent ?

A 2
3. dire quelle équipe va gagner et expliquer pourquoi ?
4. dire quelle équipe va perdre et expliquer pourquoi ?

→ Go to your WB p. 132

3 Speak
Join the team

ton objectif Devenir capitaine d'une équipe de sport.

Be going to.

Tu veux devenir capitaine d'une équipe de sport. Présente-toi, puis explique ce que tu vas faire pour l'équipe.
Es-tu capable de :

A1+
1. donner des informations sur ton identité : nom, âge, nationalité, capacités, goûts ?

A 2
2. expliquer tes intentions pour ce club ?

→ Go to your WB p. 133

2 Read
A great tournament

ton objectif Comprendre un court article de presse.

Will. Le comparatif.

Who Will Win the Australian Tennis Championship?
Federer, Nadal?

By Bill Measlow

The 2012 Australian Open will take place in Melbourne from January 18-31, 2012. It is the first of the four great tennis tournaments.
Roger Federer won the men's final of the French Open. Now Federer has a total of 14 titles for his career. He is more experienced but is he better than Nadal?
Does Rafael Nadal have a legitimate chance of taking Federer's title? He is five years younger than Federer! He has a good chance of catching Federer up!

Lis ce document avec attention.
Es-tu capable de :

A1
1. dire de quel type de document il s'agit ?
2. dire de quel sport il s'agit ?

A 2
3. dire quand, où et avec qui aura lieu la rencontre ?
4. donner les atouts de chaque joueur ?

→ Go to your WB p. 132

4 Write
My hero

ton objectif Imagine une rencontre avec ton sportif préféré.

Les superlatifs. *Will*.

Écris ce que tu feras si tu rencontres ton sportif préféré.
Es-tu capable de :

A1+
1. présenter le joueur que tu rencontreras ?

A 2
2. donner des informations sur la date et le lieu de votre rencontre ?
3. imaginer ce qu'il / elle fera lors de cette rencontre ?
4. imaginer ce que tu feras ou ne feras pas ?

→ Go to your WB p. 133

Discovery

Brits love sports

CD CLASSE

Hi guys! I'm Emma! I love sports and I'm going to be a sports reporter. Here are some of my favourites.

Team sports

Rugby
Rugby originated from Rugby school in Warwickshire. The best rugby teams compete in the Super League final each September.

Football
Football is our most popular sport. Some of England's football teams are world famous.

Cricket
Cricket is played on village greens and in cities on Sundays from April to August.

Outdoor sports

Polo
It is played on horseback between two teams of four players.
It is the oldest of equestrian sports.

Golf
Scotland is the home of golf.
There are over 400 golf courses in Scotland alone.

Tennis
The world's most famous tennis tournament is Wimbledon near London.

Athletics

The London Marathon is very popular.
The race begins at Blackheath, before crossing the River Thames at Tower Bridge and finally ends at The Mall, in front of Buckingham Palace.

School sports

At school, girls prefer playing hockey.

Olympics Games in London

The 2012 Summer Olympic Games will be held in London from 27 July to 12 August 2012, followed by the 2012 Paralympic Games from 29 August to 9 September.

Quiz time

Guess what sport it is!

1. It is played in school and it has similarities with baseball.
2. If you play this game you'll need an oval ball.
3. It's a very popular race in London.
4. If you can ride a horse, try this sport.
5. It's the favourite British sport and its most famous team is Manchester United.

FINAL TASK

Write a short magazine article about your favourite sports team or player.

1. Choose a sports team or a player you like.
2. Organize your ideas: identity, victories, projects, and predictions for next year.
3. Choose a title for your article.
4. Write 2 paragraphs showing your admiration.

B2i Print your article. Don't forget to read it before.

http://kids.yahoo.com/sports

HALLOWEEN

Video Flash DVD

Boo! Tonight is a scary night. It's October, 31st. It is Halloween night. You aren't scared, are you?

CD CLASSE

Did you know?

Halloween means "All Hallows Eve", the evening before All Saints. Halloween is a popular event in Great Britain, Ireland and America.

TRICK OR TREAT!

I love Halloween! With my friends, we wear spooky costumes and we walk in the streets by night. We knock on doors or ring bells and we say "trick or treat!". People give us sweets, fruit or money. If they don't, we play a trick on them (wrapping[1] their car with toilet paper, writing on the windows with spray shaving cream[2]...).

1. en emballant **2.** mousse à raser

DRESSING UP

Listen and guess who's who.

PUMPKINS OR JACK O'LANTERN?

Did you know?
If you put a jack o'lantern in front of your house on Halloween night it will protect you from witches.

A jack o'lantern is a pumpkin with eyes, a nose and a scary mouth. There's a candle in it.

HALLOWEEN FOOD

Typical Halloween food is nuts, popcorn, pumpkin pie and candied apples.
Children often play "bobbing for apples": they use a large basin of water with apples in it. They can't use their hands to catch the apples!
Just their mouth!

HAVE FUN! CD CLASSE

Tongue twisters

Listen to the tongue twisters.
Try to repeat them.

a. Can black bats blow bubbles?
b. If two witches watch two watches, which witch watches which watch?
c. Helen heard a horrible howling in Harry's haunted house on Halloween night.
d. Which witch wished which wicked wish?

Halloween Quiz

1. When is Halloween ?
2. What do children wear on Halloween night ?
3. Explain what « trick or treat » is.
4. Give examples of typical Halloween food.

CLASS PROJECT

My house is haunted!

1 Listen then answer the questions. CD CLASSE

a) Is it an interview? a poem? a radio message?
b) Who is speaking?
c) What is her problem?
d) Tell what happens in her house.

My school is haunted!

2 Prepare your message to Dina.

a) Write 5 facts, telling your school is haunted.
b) Mention scary creatures (people or animals).
c) Explain what you saw and heard, where? when?

Guy Fawkes

Video Flash DVD

Remember, remember
the fifth of November
Gunpowder, treason and plot.
I see no reason,
why gunpowder treason
Should ever be forgot.

CD CLASSE

Travel in time... the year is 1605, James I is the king of England.

Some people want to kill him! Listen to Guy Fawkes and the conspirators...

We must kill the king!

Fortunately for King James I, guards discovered Guy Fawkes in the cellars and took him to the Tower of London. Guy Fawkes was a prisoner at the Tower of London. Then, he was executed!

"We love Bonfire night!"

We make "Guys" and walk in the streets. We ask for money, "a penny for the Guy"! We make big bonfires[1] and burn the *Guys*! We must be careful with bonfires and fireworks! They are dangerous!

1. feu de joie

The Fireworks Safety Code

- Don't drink alcohol when you set off fireworks[1].
- Never put fireworks in your pocket.
- Always supervise children around fireworks.
- Never give sparklers[2] to children under five.
- Keep pets indoors.

1. feux d'artifice
2. cierges magiques

Guy Fawkes Quiz

1. Who was King of England in 1605?
2. Who did Guy Fawkes want to kill?
3. What do English children do on Guy Fawkes Day?

CLASS PROJECT

Create a poster about Guy Fawkes.

1. Take a large sheet of paper.
2. Copy the Guy Fawkes poem in the center.
3. Find pictures to illustrate the Guy Fawkes celebration in Great Britain.
4. Stick them around the poem.

Christmas

Video Flash DVD

Merry Christmas and Happy New Year!

Christmas dinner

At Christmas, I love being with my family. We eat a big dinner! We have lots of fun!

My Christmas Tree

I always decorate my tree with my sister. We put a lot of lights in our tree!

Did you know?

In London, every year, there is a giant Christmas tree near the statue of Lord Nelson in Trafalgar Square.

Did you know?

The first Christmas card was sent by Sir Henry Cole in 1843. Today the average person in Britain sends 50 Christmas cards every year.

I love Christmas crackers!

I love Christmas crackers! We make them with my aunt Laura. She is the specialist!

Christmas Carols

At Christmas, we always sing Christmas Carols in my school. We have fun! My favourite Christmas songs are "We Wish You a Merry Christmas", "Jingle Bells" and "Rudolph the Red-Nosed Reindeer".

A Christmas Card

Santa Quiz

1. Listen to Amy and say what her family and she do at Christmas.
2. Christmas words! Put the letters in the right order:

   arcrekc tsamcsirh lesint erte erptnes

3. How many Christmas cards do British people send every year?
4. Can you give the title of two Christmas Carols?
5. What can you use to decorate a Christmas tree?
6. What do British people traditionally eat at Christmas?

CLASS PROJECT

Group 1: Create your own Christmas Cracker

Go online and find information to create your own Christmas cracker:

http://www.oldenglishcrackers.com/make-your-own-crackers.htm

Group 2: Create your own Christmas card

1 Draw and colour a Christmas scene for the cover.

2 Inside the card, write a message for the people you love.

http://www.woodlands-junior.kent.sch.uk/CUSTOMS/Xmas/activities/webquest.html
http://www.enchantedlearning.com/crafts/christmas/treecard/

Saint Patrick's day

Video Flash DVD

March 17 is the biggest Irish festival: it's Saint Patrick's day. BEANNACHTA FILE PADRAIG ORAIBH! This is how we say "Happy Saint Patrick's Day" in Gaelic!

Did you know?

Who was Saint Patrick?
Saint Patrick crossed the sea from Britanny to Ireland six centuries ago. He arrived in Ireland and converted the Celts to Catholicism. The Irish believe Saint Patrick is their ancestor. Today, Saint Patrick's Day is one of the most celebrated festivals all over the world.

Dress in green!

Here are the 4 things you must not forget to do on Saint Patrick's day!

Send a card to someone you love!

"Happy Saint Patrick's day!"

Hi Moira,
I wish you a happy Saint Patrick's day! Maybe I'll see you in the parade. What are you going to wear? I'm going to paint my face in green! Have fun and enjoy your lunch with your family. See you soon. Love. Michael.
PS: don't forget to make soda bread for the class!

Did you know?

In the USA only there are 34Million people of Irish descent, 8 times the population of Ireland!

Have a traditional meal with your family!

Saint Patrick's day is the Irish equivalent of Thanksgiving. People spend time with their families and have a traditional lunch: Irish stew or Salmon and soda bread.

Join the parade!

March 17 is the biggest Irish carnival in the world!

Irish Soda Bread is the traditional cake. It's easy to make with only four ingredients: flour, baking soda, salt and buttermilk.

Ingredients

- 3 cups of flour
- 1 1/2 teaspoons of baking soda
- 1 1/2 teaspoons of salt
- 1 1/2 cups of buttermilk
- 1 cup of raisins

Preparation

Preheat oven to 375 degrees. In a large bowl, **mix** the baking soda, the flour and the salt. **Incorporate** the buttermilk little by little until you obtain a soft dough[1]. **Work** the dough with your hands. Place it in the oven. Let it bake[2] for 45 minutes. The soda bread is ready when it has a golden colour.

1. pâte **2.** cuire

Saint Patrick Quiz

1. When did Saint Patrick arrive in Ireland?
2. What can you eat on Saint Patrick's day?
3. Can you find the answer to this riddle: Why do frogs love Saint Patrick's day?

CLASS PROJECT

Imagine your costume to join the parade on St Patrick's day

1 Decide on different elements:

a) Which colour will be dominant?

b) Will you dress up as an Irish character or not?

c) Make a list of the different parts of your costume.

2 Now, draw your costume as you imagine it. Don't forget funny details!

Alice's Adventures in Wonderland

The White Rabbit

It's a sunny afternoon. Alice and her sister are sitting by the river. Alice's sister is reading a book with no pictures. "I don't like books without any pictures", Alice thinks. She is sleepy[1].

Just then she sees a white rabbit. He looks at his watch[2] and says, "I'm late!" "How strange! A rabbit with a watch!", Alice thinks. She follows[3] the rabbit across the grass and into a big hole[4]. She falls[5] slowly down the hole. [...] Alice sees the rabbit again and follows him. He is running around a hall with a lot of doors. Then she sees a glass table[6] with a small key on it. She takes the key and tries to open the doors, but she can't.

Then she sees a very small door and opens it. There's a beautiful garden. "I want to go into that garden," Alice thinks, "but I'm too big." She puts the keys on the glass table and sees a bottle on it. It says "DRINK ME" on the bottle. She takes the bottle and drinks it all. "Oh, how strange!" she says. "Now I'm very small and I can go into the garden." But the door is closed and the key is on the table. She's too small and she can't get the key! She is very sad and starts to cry[7]. Alice sees a small glass box under the table. Inside the box there is a cake with the words "EAT ME" on it. "I'm going to eat it" says Alice. "Perhaps I can grow[8] and take the key from the table." She eats the cake and suddenly she becomes big.[...] She takes the key and goes to the door to the garden. But she is too big and can't go in. She sits down and starts to cry again.[...]

Suddenly she sees the White Rabbit again. He's wearing a lovely jacket and he has got white gloves[9] in one hand and flowers in the other. "Oh, the Duchess is going to be very angry because I'm late!" says the White Rabbit. "Excuse me, sir…," says Alice. The White Rabbit is afraid and runs away. His white gloves fall to the floor. Alice looks at her hand and she is suddenly wearing one of the White Rabbit's gloves. "Oh, no," she says, "I'm becoming small again!"[…]

Adapted from *Alice's Adventures in Wonderland*, Lewis Carroll, 1871.

1. envie de dormir 2. sa montre 3. suit 4. trou 5. tombe 6. table en verre 7. pleurer 8. grandir 9. des gants

1 Read the text: who are the two heroes?

2 Where is the girl? Put the pictures in the right order.

3 What are the three magical objects?

4 Where are they?

5 Why are they magical?

Class project

Imagine a story called "In a magic house".

1. Imagine two characters (a child and an animal). Make a short description.
2. Describe the different rooms of the magic house.
3. Imagine magical objects: say where they are and what your hero can do with them.

Listen and speak

Part 1 School friends

Unit 1 Back to school

Mrs Monroe: Shh, children! Listen to the headmaster!
Mr Lloyd: Good morning everyone and welcome to all Year 7 pupils! Two new teachers are at Teddington School this year: Mr Grant and Mrs Monroe. Mr Grant is a PE teacher. He's from Dublin and Mrs Monroe…
Chad: I'm so happy, Tom!
Tom: You're happy to be back at school? Are you ok, Chad?
Chad: I'm happy because we're in the same class. Hey, who's that girl?
Tom: I don't know. I think she's new. I think she's Australian.
Chad: Hey, psss, what's your name?
Scarlett: I'm Scarlett.
Chad: Are you Australian?
Scarlett: No, I'm not. I'm American.
Chad: How old …?
Mr Lloyd: What's your name young man?
Chad: I'm Chad, Sir, Chad O'Malley, O: ': M: A: L: L: E: Y.
Mr Lloyd: Well I'm Mr Lloyd, the headmaster. Remember my name LL: O: Y: D.
Now, act your age and stop chatting!

Unit 2 I love history

Mrs Preston: Patrick, can you open the window, please?
Scarlett: Sorry Mrs Preston, I'm late. Can I come in?
Mrs Preston: It's alright for today Scarlett, but don't forget the room number next time. Well, children, let's start. Let's talk about kings and queens! Can you give me the name of…the Queen of England?
Class: Queen Elizabeth!
Mrs Preston: Well. That's easy. More difficult… Can you give me the name of a Norman king…Tom! Can you repeat the question?
Tom: … a Norman king!
Scarlett: William the Conqueror!
Mrs Preston: Congratulations Scarlett!
Tom *(aside)*: Wow!
Mrs Preston: And now question for the champions. Can you tell me who this man is? He had six wives. His first wife was Catherine of Aragon, his second wife was Ann Boleyn and…
Patrick: Miss… Miss… I know! I know!
Mrs Preston: Yes Patrick?
Patrick: It's King George.
Mrs Preston: No, it isn't. Scarlett! Can you answer?
Scarlett: Henry VIII.
Mrs Preston: Brilliant! Join the school history club!
Tom: She's incredible!

Part 2 Home, sweet home

Unit 3 Come in!

Chad: You've got a great house Tom. Have you got a TV in your room?
Tom: No, I haven't but I've got a computer and a lot of games. My room is upstairs.
Chad: Cool! Let's go!
Chad: Who is this ?
Tom: Shh! My little sister, Zoe. She's got a new CD. Have you got a sister?
Chad: No, I haven't. I've got a brother.
Tom: You're so lucky!
Chad: Wow! You've got a lot of DVDs and oh… lots of books! What's that? *Romeo and Juliet…*
Tom: Well, er… Have you got any pets?
Chad: No I haven't. What about you?
Tom: I've got hamsters and Zoe's got a cat, a terrible cat, his name's Tiger and he's not nice!
Chad: Where are your hamsters?
Tom: There! On my desk, next to the computer.
Chad: How many hamsters have you got?
Tom: Oh! Just two. This is Romeo…
Chad: and I suppose… this is Juliet. Ah, ah ah!!

Unit 4 A garden party

Tom: Good evening Mrs Williams! I'm Tom, and this is Chad. We're Scarlett's friends.
Mrs Williams: Hello… Good evening Tom, good evening Chad. How are you? … Come on in…
Tom: We're fine, thank you.
Mrs Williams: Come into the kitchen.
Scarlett: Hi there! Come on, let's go outside in the garden.

Tom: Oh… wow…a garden party! …
Chad: I love barbecue! Yummy!… Sausages, chicken, wow! Crisps, tomato salad… orange juice, Coke!! and I'm so hungry! And so thirsty!
Tom: So Scarlett, tell me, do you like your life in England?
Scarlett: Oh, yes I do! I love it! I've got lots of friends now! It's great! But… I miss my dad.
Tom: You miss your dad? What do you mean?
Scarlett: Well, see, I live here in Kingston with my mom, but my dad doesn't live in England. He lives and works in New York.
Tom: Chad! Look at your plate!! five sausages! Chicken and crisps! Pff… You eat too much!
Chad: Huh… I don't care! It's not a problem! I am an athlete!
Chad: Well, it's true! I play football! Basket ball! Tennis! And I do gymnastics every day!
Tom: You don't do gymnastics!
Chad: Oh, yes, I do. Look!
Tom and Scarlett: Chad, watch out! Your plate!
Chad: Ouch! Oh noo, my food!
Scarlett: Oops…Chad, you're a real star!

Part 3 Let's take a tour

Unit 6 A scary visit

Chad: Oh no! I haven't got the map!
Tom, Zoe, Scarlett: Chaaaaad!
Zoe: Tom, call Mum.
Tom: Hi Mum, we're in London. We haven't got a map. We are at the British Museum. Can you tell us the way to the Tower of London?
Mum: Yeah, right… You must go straight on to Kingsway; then you must turn left on to High Holborn; go straight on and then you must turn right on to Farrington Road; then you must turn left on to Fleet Street and go straight on to Cannon street.
Tom: Ok, thank you mum. Ok let's go! I'm excited! We must hurry up!

At the Tower

Chad: Watch out Tom, the birds! They are dangerous!
Tom: No they aren't. They can't fly.
Zoe: Look up there! I can see two ghosts in the window!
Tom: Come on Zoe. Ghosts don't exist!
Zoe: Yes they do! And they can run and they can fly!
Children: AAAAAAH!
Guide: The visit of the prison begins in five minutes… Please wait next to the tree. Visitors mustn't bring drinks or food and mustn't use their mobile phones.
Chad: Wow! Great!
Zoe: It's dark, I'm scared!
Chad: Look, what's this?
Zoe: A ring! Maybe it's a Queen's ring!
Scarlett: Maybe it's Queen Elizabeth's ring!
Chad: No, it's plastic…
Scarlett: It's beautiful, can I have it?
Tom: Sure, a souvenir from the Tower of London.

Part 4 Family fun

Unit 7 What a family!

Chad: Hey guys, listen to this: Do you want to go to a picnic in Canterbury with me and my family on Saturday?
Scarlett: Oh cool but… No, I don't think I can come: I have my guitar lessons on Saturdays.
Chad: Oh, come on… My aunt Mary can play with you! She plays the guitar and she sings all the time! Come on! Please Scarlett… please!
Scarlett: Well… ok!
Chad: What about you, Tom?
Tom: Well, on Saturdays, I often play rugby… you know…
Chad: Well, you can play with my uncle Paul. He plays rugby in a club! He is soooo good!
Tom: Ok, ok, all right…
Chad: Yess! This is soooo cool! A picnic together! And we can visit the cathedral too! It's great!
But listen… there's a little problem: the food! My parents only eat organic food. My mother is a vegetarian. She doesn't eat meat. She sometimes eats eggs, but not often… And she always drinks tomato juice… She thinks fruit and vegetables are your friends! She always says *"An apple a day keeps the doctor away!"*
Tom: Oh, really?
Chad: Yeah…, and my brother and my dad are crazy about jelly! They eat jelly every day.
Scarlett: What a family! Err… Can I… bring crisps?
Chad: Well, sure, but my parents never eat crisps. They think crisps are not healthy… crisps are … the enemy!
Scarlett & Tom: Oh…

Unit 8 A picnic in Canterbury

Mrs O'Malley: Oh what a mess! Wait, whose carrot juice is this?
Mr. O'Malley: It's my carrot juice, darling.
Chad's brother: Mum, I want my jelly...
Mrs O'Malley: Wait a minute! You must eat your vegetables first...And whose...Oh, whose, whose crisps are these?
Scarlett: They are mine Mrs O'Malley.
Chad's brother: Mum, I want crisps too! I don't want vegetables! I want ham and I want sausages! I want chocolate cake!
Mrs O'Malley: Oh, stop it! Eat your carrot and be quiet! ...Where's uncle Paul?
Scarlett: He's in the cathedral with Chad and Tom.

Inside the cathedral
Chad: Wow, look... this is beautiful!
Tom: Hey! Look over there! The Black Prince! It's very impressive!
Paul: Come on! I want to show you something... There...
Chad: Look, the swords!
Chad and Tom: Wow...
Paul: This is where Thomas Beckett was executed!
Tom and Chad: Wow, yeah look in 1170...
Chad: Look a passage... to go down into the Crypt! Wow... let's go...
Paul: Yes... But children! Be very careful... the stairs are...

Part 5 Show time

Unit 10 Time to act

Mrs Monroe: Now children, you must choose your roles for my new musical: Fame! Who wants to be Jenny?
Scarlett: Oh Mrs Monroe, I'd love to be Jenny. I can dance very well!
Mrs Monroe: All right Scarlett. And who wants to be Marco?
Tom and Chad: I do, Mrs Monroe!
Chad: Mrs Monroe, I think I am better than Tom. First, I can dance better!
Tom: Oh!
Chad: And I look better. I am taller and I am stronger. I am more athletic and I am more attractive.
Tom: But Mrs Monroe, I'm more intelligent than Chad! I've got a better memory and I work harder! I will learn my part very well...
Chad: Oh for sure Tom, you are more romantic! Why don't you play Denise ? I'm sure you are better at "ballet".
Mrs Monroe: Stop! Stop! Now Scarlett, choose your partner!
Scarlett: Well... I think Chad is funnier, and he dances very well, but... in my opinion, Tom's a better actor... Sorry Chad.

Unit 11 Getting ready for the show

Mrs Monroe: Children! You're too slow! We must get ready for the show! What are you all doing? Tom, what are you doing? Come out of the fitting room now!
Tom: I'm coming Mrs Monroe, I'm putting on my trousers! But they are too long! I can't walk!
Mrs Monroe: What about you Chad?
Chad: I can't wear this pink shirt Mrs Monroe! It's too tight! Please, please Mrs Monroe, can we buy the red shirt? It's more comfortable!
Mrs Monroe: How much is that red shirt?
Chad: Errrr... twenty-four pounds ninety-nine...
Mrs Monroe: Argh! It's far too expensive! Take the pink shirt, it's only four pounds. Now where's Scarlett? What is she doing? Are you trying on your dress?
Chad: She's talking on the phone Mrs Monroe.
Mrs Monroe: Scarlett? Are you really speaking on the phone? Give me your mobile phone immediately.
Scarlett: Sorry Mrs Monroe but...
Mrs Monroe: I'm not joking! Hello? No, I'm not Scarlett's friend! I'm Scarlett's teacher! Yes we are working! No we are not at school; we are in a shop, we are buying the costumes for the show! What? No we're not having fun! Sorry? You're Scarlett's father? Oops, sorry Sir!

Part 6 Across the sea

Unit 13 Off to Ireland

Tom: Mrs Faye Darlington, thank you so much for inviting us to Ireland.
Scarlett: Oh yes, thank you, it's so exciting! Chad is so lucky to have a great-aunt like you!
Rose: You're welcome my darling. Ah! It's so nice to be travelling on a ship, on the Irish Sea...
Scarlett: Oh, I can see the coast!

Chad: Wow!
Tom: Cool! Ireland!
Rose: Calm down, children... Let me tell you about Ireland... and my first love story. His name was Danny, he...
Chad: Oh come on! We'd like to hear about Ireland!
Rose: Ok! What would you like to visit?
Scarlett: I'd like to see magic castles!
Tom: I'd like to see lakes!
Chad: I'd like to go to a pub... Hahaha... and listen to the music.
Rose: Oh! I know, we should visit Bunratty castle. It's a great castle! And we should go to Connemara, the lakes are beautiful; oh yes I know... we should go to the Aran Islands; they are magic. I remember... with Danny...
Chad: Auntie Rose, would you like some tea? I'll go and get some for you.
Rose: Oh, what a nice boy you are! Yes please, I'd like some tea and I'd like some cucumber sandwiches. And look Ireland! I can see Rosslare harbour!
Chad: Let's go to the upper deck! Auntie, come with us! Hurry up!
Rose: Slowly, slowly my little darling...Who do you think I am, Spiderwoman?

Unit 14 The magic island

Scarlett: Oh, Rose, your house is so beautiful! The lake is so nice...
Rose: I lived in this house when I was young...
My family bought it a century ago.
Chad: A century ago! Wow! How old are you?
Rose: I'm just eighty-three years old! I wasn't born a century ago, you silly boy! I'm not a dinosaur!
Chad: Hey auntie, look! There's a man in the garden.
Rose: But... wait a minute! Hey, it's Danny!
Danny: Rose, still so beautiful!
Rose: Oh Danny! ... Children! Come here! Chad, Tom, Scarlett! This is Danny, my first boyfriend!
Chad & co: Ooooh!
Danny: Yes, we met in this garden, sixty-five years, six months, and twelve days ago... I never forgot that moment... When did you arrive in Ireland?
Rose: We arrived two days ago. Danny, when did I last see you? We were so happy together! Then, one day, you disappeared... Why did you disappear? Where did you go?
Danny: My family was so poor! We had no money! We had no food! Life was too difficult! And then, one day, I found two gold coins in a cave near the sea. With the coins, I bought a ticket and I went to America.
Scarlett, Tom and Chad: To America!
Danny: And look, Rose! I still have this photo! Do you remember?
Rose: Oh, the picture by the sea...
Scarlett, Tom and Chad: Oooooh!

Part 7 Challenges

Unit 15 Who's going to win?

Steve: So, Tom, ready for the defeat of your live? You, chickens! We're going to beat you! You hear?
Tom: Yeah, sure! We won the match last Saturday!
Steve: Er, you were lucky! I was ill...But this time you are not going to win! I'm faster than you and rugby is my sport!
Tom: Well, my players are smarter and stronger than yours!
Steve: I am faster than you! And look at Dan! He hasn't got his glasses on. I'm sure he's going to fall over! Ah! Ah! Ah! We're going to crush you!
Tom: Oh you... I'm going to....
Scarlett: Don't listen to him, Tom! You know he's stupid!
"And now Ladies and Gentlemen, Kingston Secondary versus..."
Scarlett: I'm sure you're going to win. You're my hero!
Chad: Tom, pass me the ball!
Scarlett: Be careful, Chad! Behind you! Run! Oh dear! No!
Chad: Ouuuuuucchhh... my ear!

Exercise Bank

CD ÉLÈVE Audio-Rom

Part 1 School friends

1 Complète les phrases suivantes avec le mot qui convient.

headmaster – classroom – playground – uniform – pupils – pencils – teacher

a. We are 800 … at school.
b. The maths … is Mrs Roberts.
c. It's 10 o'clock: my friends are in the ….
d. Mr Truman is the … of the school.
e. I've got ten … in my pencil case.
f. Everyone in school wears a ….
g. We have lessons in the ….

2 Complète les phrases avec la forme verbale qui convient.

a. Hi, my name *(is/be)* Harry. I *(have/am)* 12 years old and I *(are/am)* a pupil at Teddington School.
b. I've got two sisters who *(are/is)* also at school, but they *(isn't/aren't)* in my class.
c. Mrs Williams *(are/is)* my art teacher and art *(is/are)* my favourite class.

3 Remets les lettres dans l'ordre pour compléter les phrases.

a. Can I … a question? K A S
b. At night, you … . E P E L S
c. In the morning, you … . E A W K P U
d. You … with a pen. T I E W R
e. Shut up! Don't … . T L K A
f. Shh! Please … . N L T S E I

4 Remets les mots dans l'ordre pour faire des phrases à l'impératif.

a. door / open / ! / the
b. ! / a / me / pencil / give
c. the / answer / ! / question
d. with / help / ! / me / homework / my
e. your / name / tell / me / !
f. books / ! / open / your

Part 2 Home, sweet home

1 Recompose les mots pour terminer les phrases.

a. I sleep in my … D B E
b. My rabbit is my favourite… TEP
c. The bedrooms are… S S U T A P R I
d. I watch TV in the… N L G I V I - M O O R
e. We cook in the… T E K C I N H
f. On my desk, there is a… E C T O R M U P

2 Complète cette conversation en choisissant la forme verbale qui convient.

Julie: *(Has you got/Have you got)* a TV in your room?
Thomas: No, I *(haven't/haven't got)*, but I *('ve got/'s got)* a computer.
Julie: My brother *(is got/'s got)* a TV in his room and he *('ve got/'s got)* a lot of DVDs.
Thomas: *(Has he got/Have he got)* "Twilight"?
Julie: Yes, he *(has got/has)*.

3 Observe les dessins et trouve les mots qui correspondent.

a. 

b. 

c. 

d. 

e. 

f. 

g. 

4 Complète les phrases avec la forme verbale qui convient.

you work – like – I'm – do you – I live – I do

You: … live in London?
Harry: No, … in Manchester.

You: And do you ... Manchester?
Harry: Yes ... . I like it very much.
You: Where do ...?
Harry: I work in a studio. ... a photographer.

Part 3 Let's take a tour

1 Recompose les mots emmêlés à partir des indices proposés.

a. The birds at the Tower of London. R S A E V N
b. An insect with eight legs. E P I R S D
c. Gives the time. K C L C O
d. On a king's head. O N C W R
e. A king's house. T L C A E S

2 Complète les phrases suivantes en choisissant la forme qui convient.

a. *(How much/How many)* is this souvenir?
b. *(How much/How many)* T-shirts have you got?
c. *(How much/How many)* mugs are there?
d. *(How much/How many)* guidebooks do you want?
e. *(How much/How many)* are the pencils?
f. *(How much/How many)* castles are there in London?

3 Lis les indices et complète les phrases avec la partie du corps qui convient.

a. You put food in your ... .
b. You hear with your ... .
c. At the end of your hands: ... .
d. You walk with your ... .
e. Between your eyes and your mouth: ... .
f. Your hair is on your ... .
g. At the end of your feet: ... .

4 Complète les phrases suivantes en choisissant la forme verbale qui convient.

a. In the Tower, you *(can/mustn't)* see the Crown Jewels.
b. You *(mustn't/must)* listen to the guide.
c. During the visit, you *(must/can't)* use your phone.
d. You *(mustn't/must)* eat snacks in the souvenir shop.
e. First, you *(can't/must)* buy a ticket.
f. You *(must/mustn't)* touch the torture instruments.

Part 4 Family fun

1 Repère l'intrus.

a. uncle – singer – aunt – grandfather
b. sweets – cheese – every – juice
c. guitar – baker – doctor – teacher
d. never – always – often – aunt
e. breakfast – mother – lunch – dinner

2 Remets les mots dans l'ordre.

a. we / at 8 o'clock / always / have breakfast
b. sometimes / organic food / I / eat
c. hungry / is / always / Chad
d. Scarlett / drinks / never / carrot juice
e. jelly / I / eat / never
f. are / picnics / fun / often

3 Lis les indices et complète la phrase.

a. Tomato, carrot or orange ... .
b. Fish and ... .
c. Carrots, broccoli and potatoes are all ... .
d. Very bad for your teeth! ...
e. A ... and tomato sandwich.
f. The sandwiches are in the picnic ... .

4 Complète les phrases suivantes avec l'article qui convient.

the – Ø – an – a

a. ... picnic is in the basket.
b. ... chips are not very healthy.
c. Do you want apple?
d. Is it organic tomato?
e. Pass me cheese sandwich, please.
f. I like sweets.

5 Remets les lettres dans l'ordre pour compléter les phrases.

a. You can play tennis in the ... . K A P R
b. You can post letters at the ... . O P T S F F E I O C
c. You can buy books at a ... . P O S O K O B H
d. You can buy bread at the ... . E Y K B R A
e. You can see films at the ... . N M C E I A
f. You can swim in a ... . M M G I S N W I L O O P

CD ÉLÈVE Audio-Rom

6 Complète les phrases suivantes avec la forme verbale qui convient.

was – didn't eat – were – didn't see – drank

a. Chad and Tom ... in the cathedral.
b. They ... the crypt.
c. The children ... a soda.
d. Scarlett ... carrots.
e. The family ... crazy!

Part 5 Show time

1 Lis les définitions et trouve les mots correspondants.

a. not small.
b. not stupid.
c. not short.
d. not old.
e. not fast.
f. not fat.
g. not funny.

2 Observe les adjectifs et complète le tableau.

big	...
...	funnier
good	...
...	taller
...	worse
strong	...

3 Recompose les mots à partir des indices proposés pour trouver des noms de vêtements.

a. On your feet. E S H S O
b. Inside your shoes. O S K C S
c. For the winter. T A C O
d. For girls. RSIKT
e. With two legs! S E O U T R S R
f. On your head. PAC

4 Associe chaque question à la réponse qui convient.

a. What are you doing?	1. He's going to the cinema.
b. Where is he going?	2. No, it's snowing.
c. Are you crying?	3. Yes, are you coming with me?
d. Are you going shopping?	4. I'm calling my friend.
e. Is it raining?	5. No, I'm joking.

5 Repère l'intrus.

a. actor / dress / dancer / singer
b. clothes / star / fame / success
c. act / sing / attractive / dance
d. spectators / audience / fans / fashion

6 Complète cette conversation en choisissant le pronom personnel qui convient.

Ed: Can you help *(I/me)* with my script?
Emma: Of course! Don't you know *(it/him)*?
Ed: No, but *(we/us)* have to learn it for tomorrow.
Emma: Mrs Mason is fantastic. I want to be perfect for *(she/her)*.
Ed: Yes, I know. *(She/Her)* is working very hard.
Emma: But *(we/us)* have to work hard too!!

Part 6 Across the sea

1 Complète les phrases suivantes avec le moyen de transport qui convient.

bus – bicycle – coast – plane – car – ship

a. I've got a new ..., but it's still difficult to push the pedals!
b. We would like to rent a ..., a Ford Fiesta, please.
c. I see my friends every morning on the ... .
d. British Airways, a British airline, have a new ... .
e. The Titanic was an enormous ... .
f. Look! I can see the beaches on the ... !

2 Lis les indices et complète les phrases.

a. 100 years is a ... .
b. A princess lives in a ... .
c. Loch Ness is a ... .
d. 365 days is a ... .
e. A ... is a small mountain.
f. 30 days is a ... .
g. A ship sails on the ... .

3 Associe chaque question à la réponse qui correspond.

a. Why did you laugh?	1. Because I was ill.
b. Why were you absent?	2. In my pocket!
c. Where did you go?	3. I'm not telling you!
d. Where was your telephone?	4. Fish and chips.
e. What did you eat?	5. Because it was funny!
f. What was the answer?	6. To the cinema.

4 Remets les mots dans l'ordre pour faire des phrases exclamatives.

a. big / What / ship! / a
b. old! / My / bicycle / so / is
c. so / bus / This / is / slow!
d. car! / expensive / an / What
e. train / comfortable! / The / so / is
f. fantastic / What / plane! / a

Part 7 Challenges

1 Recompose les phrases à partir des indices proposés pour trouver des noms de sports.

a. A person who swims is a ... M E S I M W R
b. On my bicycle, I like ... G Y I C N C L
c. A person who plays tennis is a tennis ... R Y E L A P
d. If you like shooting arrows, you like ... R Y E C A H R
e. A person who skies is a ... E S I K R
f. On my horse, I go ... D I N R G I

2 Lis les phrases suivantes et dis si l'action est : 1) en cours ou si 2) elle va se réaliser.

a. They're going to play tennis.
b. I'm going to cycle to school.
c. He's dribbling the ball.
d. She's going to ice-skate.
e. They're listening to the coach.
f. He's scoring a goal.

3 Lis les indices et complète les phrases.

a. A competition between two teams.
b. Each side of the ..., there is a goalpost.
c. There are 11 players in a football ...
d. The winner of the competition.
e. The ... was 3 – 0.
f. All the ... were happy because their team won.

4 Complète les phrases suivantes avec le superlatif qui convient.

a. He's fast! → He's the ... player in the team.
b. We're strong! → We're the ... team in the tournament.
c. They're good! → They're the ... team in the school.
d. She's beautiful! → She's the ... girl in the school.
e. She's bad! → She's the ... swimmer in the race.
f. This is amazing! → This is the ... match of the tournament.

Test d'évaluation

1 Compréhension de l'oral

Écoute ce garçon.

A1
1. Relève les informations concernant son identité :
a) nom, prénom **b)** nationalité **c)** domicile (ville, pays)

A1+
2. Relève les informations concernant :
a) ce qu'il aime **b)** ce qu'il n'aime pas

3. Relève les informations concernant :
a) son meilleur ami **b)** ses frères et sœurs **c)** ses parents **d)** son animal familier

4. Relève les informations concernant sa maison, sa chambre.

2 Compréhension de l'écrit

Lis le document.

A1
1. Dis :
a) de quel type de document il s'agit.
b) où se situe ce lieu (adresse, ville).

A1+
2. Donne des informations pratiques (horaires, prix).

3. Fais une description de ce que l'on peut visiter sur ce site.

A2
4. Explique en détail ce qu'est le *Ghost Tour*.

5. Explique l'expression « Dover Castle – 2000 Years of History ».

Welcome to Dover Castle
2000 Years of History

Canons Gate Road,
Dover, CT16 1HU
01304 211067

Opening times
30 January – 31 March
10:00 – 4:00
1 April – 30 September
10:00 – 6:00
1 October – 29 January
10:00 – 4:00
(Closed Tuesdays & Wednesdays in Nov/Dec/Jan)

Prices
Adult – £13.90
Child – £7.00
Family ticket – £34.80

THE ROMAN LIGHTHOUSE
Come and see this beautiful monument! It is a monument from the Roman period. The Romans built it in around 100 AD.

THE ANGLO-SAXON CHURCH
Visit the church of St Mary in Castro, one of the most beautiful Anglo-Saxon churches in the country!

THE GREAT TOWER – THE KEEP
The Great Tower of Dover Castle was built in 1172 by Henry II, one of the most powerful English kings of all time.
It is the most spectacular building in one of Europe's most spectacular castles. Walk inside the tower and discover medieval life.

Spooky!
Take the Ghost Tour. Prepare to be spooked with our ghostly guided tours.
Take a night tour of the site and discover the dark side of Dover Castle! Get ready to meet lots of ghosts in every corner of the castle!

Duration: Approx. 3 hours. Tour starts at 5:30 pm
Only in January and February
£25 per person (includes a light meal of soup and bread)
For information call **0870 333 1181**

Don't forget to visit the gift shop for souvenirs
Visit us at **http://www.english-heritageshop.org.uk**

3 Expression orale

Tu as reçu la brochure touristique du château de Douvres. Tu dois présenter ce lieu à ta classe.

A1

1. **Présente-toi brièvement à tes camarades.**
2. **Présente le sujet de ton intervention.**

A1+

3. **Présente le château.**
   a) Dis ce qu'il y a à visiter.
   b) Parle de ce qu'il est possible d'y faire.

A2

4. **Explique pourquoi tu penses que ce monument est intéressant, et pourquoi tu veux le visiter.**

4 Expression écrite

Tu viens d'arriver dans une nouvelle école à Londres. Tes professeurs te demandent de rédiger un court texte pour le journal du collège dans lequel tu te présentes à tes nouveaux camarades. Rédige quelques phrases

A1

1. **pour te présenter en précisant**
   a) ton nom, ton prénom.
   b) ton âge.
   c) ta nationalité.
   d) ta ville, ton pays.

A1+

2. **pour décrire ta famille**
   a) tes frères et sœurs.
   b) tes parents.
3. **pour parler de tes goûts**
4. **pour décrire ta maison en France.**

A2

5. **Rédige un paragraphe pour dire ce qui te plait particulièrement dans la ville de Londres en parlant**
   a) des habitudes de vie anglaises (nourriture…).
   b) de la vie à Londres (les monuments, les transports…).

Précis grammatical

LE GROUPE NOMINAL

1 Les noms communs

• En anglais tous les **noms communs** prennent un **s** au **pluriel**, à part quelques exceptions :

– **les noms invariables**

→ *fruit* → *fish* → *sheep* → *hair*

– **les pluriels irréguliers**

→ *child* → *children*
→ *woman* → *women*
→ *mouse* → *mice*
→ *man* → *men*
→ *foot* → *feet*

• Les objets et les parties du corps n'ont pas de genre. Ils ne sont ni masculins ni féminins et on s'y réfère avec le pronom ***it***. On dit qu'ils sont neutres.

2 Les interrogatifs *what, where, who, how, why*

Tu utilises les pronoms ou les adverbes interrogatifs pour poser des questions.

what?	where?	who?	why?	how?
= quoi ? *What's this?*	= où ? *Where is the post office?*	= qui ? *Who's that girl?*	= pourquoi ? *Why is Chad angry?*	= comment ? *How are you today?*

⚠ Tu utilises ***how old*** pour poser une question sur l'âge d'une personne.

→ ***How old** are you? I'm 11.*

3 *How much* et *how many*

• Tu utilises ***how many*** **+ nom pluriel** pour poser une question sur une **quantité**.

→ ***How many** DVDs have you got?*

• Tu utilises ***how much*** **+ *is/are*** pour demander le **prix** d'un ou plusieurs objets.

→ ***How much** is this DVD? **How much** are these shoes?*

4 Les articles *a/an, the, Ø*

• Tu utilises ***a*** devant un **nom singulier** qui est **un élément parmi d'autres.**

→ *Look, there's **a** cat in the garden!*
→ *Can I have **a** biscuit, please?*

⚠ Devant un son voyelle, ***a*** devient ***an*** pour faire la liaison. → *an apple*

⚠ Devant la lettre « **h** » on utilise l'article ***a***, sauf quand le « **h** » est muet.

→ *a hospital* → *an hour*

⚠ le son [ju] est un son consonne en anglais.

→ *a European* → *a Union*

• Devant un **nom pluriel**, ***a*** ou ***an*** est remplacé par l'article **Ø**.

→ *Look, there are **cats** in the garden!*

• Tu utilises ***the*** devant un nom **singulier** ou **pluriel dont tu as déjà parlé** où qui est **bien déterminé**.

→ *Look at **the** cat! She's running after a mouse!*

⚠ Il n'y a pas d'article devant les noms propres, sauf les noms de pays composés de plusieurs états.

→ *France, Spain, Great Britain, **the** United Kingdom, **the** United States*

• Il n'y a **pas d'article** :

– pour parler d'un ensemble ou d'une catégorie générale.

→ *Cats love milk*

– devant un nom propre singulier suivi d'un génitif.

→ *Mark's girlfriend*

5 Les pronoms personnels

• Tu utilises le pronom personnel ***I*** pour **parler de toi**, ***you*** pour désigner la ou des personne(s) **à qui tu t'adresses**, et ***he/she/it/we/they*** pour **remplacer les noms et éviter les répétitions**.

sujets	compléments
I	*me*
you	*you*
he/she/it	*him/her/it*
we	*us*
you	*you*
they	*them*

6 Les possessifs

adjectifs possessifs	pronoms possessifs
It's ***my*** *book.*	*It's* ***mine****.*
It's ***your*** *book.*	*It's* ***yours****.*
It's ***her*** *book.*	*It's* ***hers****.*
It's ***his*** *book.*	*It's* ***his****.*
They're ***your*** *books.*	*They're* ***yours****.*
They're ***our*** *books.*	*They're* ***ours****.*
They're ***their*** *books.*	*They're* ***theirs****.*

• Tu utilises les **adjectifs possessifs** pour dire **à qui appartient** un objet.

• Ce n'est pas l'objet mais le possesseur qui détermine le choix entre ***his*** et ***her***.

→ *This is David's car. It's* ***his*** *car.*
→ *This is Alison's car. It's* ***her*** *car.*

• Tu utilises les **pronoms possessifs** pour **remplacer** un groupe nominal composé d'un adjectif possessif et d'un nom.

7 Les adjectifs démonstratifs *this, that, these, those*

• Tu utilises les adjectifs démonstratifs **pour désigner un objet** ou **quelqu'un**.

	singulier	pluriel
+ proche • dans l'espace ou le temps • affectivement	***this*** → *Look at* ***this*** *photo.* → *I love* ***this*** *man.*	***these*** → *Look at* ***these*** *photos.* → *I love* ***these*** *people.*
+ éloigné • dans l'espace ou le temps • affectivement	***that*** → *Look at* ***that*** *mountain.* → *I hate* ***that*** *boy!*	***those*** → *Look at* ***those*** *stars.* → *I hate* ***those*** *people.*

8 Le génitif *'s* et *whose*

• Tu utilises le **génitif *'s*** pour **établir** :

– **un lien de possession entre une personne et un objet.** → *This is Scarlett****'s*** *book.*

– **un lien social entre deux personnes.**
→ *Amanda is Patrick****'s*** *girlfriend.*

⚠ La personne de qui l'on parle est placée à gauche du génitif (contrairement au français).

⚠ Si le nom est au pluriel, on forme le génitif avec l'apostrophe sans le **s**.
→ *My friends' children* (sauf avec les pluriels irréguliers → *The children's bedroom*).

• Tu utilises ***whose*** pour demander qui est le propriétaire d'un objet. ***Whose*** est toujours suivi du nom de l'objet :
→ ***Whose*** *book is this?* ***Whose*** *shoes are these?*

9 Les adjectifs qualificatifs

• Tu utilises les **adjectifs qualificatifs** pour **qualifier une personne, un objet, un animal, une action, un événement, une pensée**…

• Les adjectifs anglais sont **invariables**, ils ne prennent jamais de **s**, même quand le nom qu'ils qualifient est au pluriel.
→ *I read three* ***good*** *books this summer.*

• Ils se placent toujours **avant** le nom qu'ils qualifient ou après **be**.
→ *She's a* ***clever*** *girl.*
→ *This girl is* ***clever****.*

10 Le comparatif

- Tu utilises un **comparatif** pour **comparer deux éléments entre eux**.
- Dans le **comparatif de supériorité,** le **premier terme** est **supérieur** au **second**.
  → *John is* ***taller*** *than Mark.*
  → *Harry Potter is* ***more interesting*** *than Dracula.*
- Lorsque tu compares deux éléments entre eux, le comparatif de supériorité est suivi de la conjonction ***than***.
  → *I think Dracula is more elegant* ***than*** *Frankenstein.*

⚠ Il existe trois **comparatifs irréguliers** :
good → ***better***
bad → ***worse***
far → ***farther***

Formation du comparatif

Adjectif **d'une syllabe**	*wild* → *wild**er***	
Adjectif de **2 syllabes** se terminant par ***-y***	*funny* → *funn**ier***	
Adjectif de **2 syllabes** se terminant par ***-er***	*clever* → *clever**er***	
Adjectif de **2 syllabes** se terminant par ***-ow***	*narrow* → *the narrow**er***	
Tous les autres adjectifs de **2 syllabes ou plus**	***more*** + *adjectif*	***more*** *elegant*

11 Le superlatif

- Tu utilises le **superlatif** pour **distinguer un élément parmi d'autres** (au moins trois).

Formation du superlatif

Adjectif **d'une syllabe**	*the wild**est***	
Adjectif de **2 syllabes** se terminant par ***-y***	*funny* → *the funn**iest***	
Adjectif de **2 syllabes** se terminant par ***–er***	*clever* → *the clever**est***	
Adjectif de **2 syllabes** se terminant par ***–ow***	*narrow* → *the narrow**est***	
Tous les autres adjectifs de **2 syllabes ou plus**	***the most*** + *adjectif*	***the most*** *elegant*

⚠ Il existe trois **superlatifs irréguliers** :
good → ***the best***
bad → ***the worst***
far → ***the farthest***

■ LE GROUPE VERBAL

12 *There is/There are*

- Tu utilises ***there is/there are*** pour **décrire ce qu'il y a dans un lieu.**

There is + ***a/an*** + **nom singulier** :
→ *There's* ***a*** *spider under the bed!*

There are + **nom pluriel** :
→ *There* ***are*** *lots of shops in my town.*

13 L'impératif

- Tu utilises l'impératif pour **donner un ordre**.

Ordre positif : base verbale + !	Ordre négatif : *Don't* + base verbale
Wait! *Come!*	*Don't wait!* *Don't run!*

Pour t'inclure dans l'ordre que tu donnes, tu utilises **let's** + **base verbale** + **!**
→ ***Let's*** *go!* ***Let's*** *run!* (Allons-y ! Courons !)

14 Be et do

• ***Be*** et ***do*** sont des verbes **auxiliaires,** c'est-à-dire qu'ils peuvent être associés à un autre verbe, dans certaines formes.

Be		Do
• auxiliaire dans la forme *be* + *V-ing* *I **am** coming.* *You **are** coming.* *He/she/it **is** coming.*	*We **are** coming.* *You **are** coming.* *They **are** coming.*	• auxiliaire dans les phrases au présent simple et au prétérit ***Do** you know Chad?* ***Did** you see the film?*

15 Have got

• Tu utilise la forme ***have got*** pour **exprimer la possession.**

Forme affirmative	Forme interrogative	Forme négative	Réponse courte
*I**'ve got** a computer.* *He**'s got** a computer.*	***Have** you **got** a computer ?* ***Has** he **got**... ?* ***Have** they **got**... ?*	*I **haven't got** a computer.* *He **hasn't got** a computer.*	*Yes, I **have**.* *No, she **hasn't**.*

⚠ Au passé, ***have got*** devient ***had got*** à toutes les personnes et aux formes affirmative et interrogative. ***Haven't*** devient ***hadn't*** à la forme négative.

16 Le présent simple

• Tu utilises le présent simple :

– pour parler des **caractéristiques** ou des **habitudes** de quelqu'un.
→ *He lives in New York.*
→ *He gets up every day at six.*

– pour parler d'un **emploi du temps.**
→ *The train leaves at 6 p.m.*
→ *We have maths at 11 a.m. on Mondays.*

• Aux **formes interrogative et négative**, le verbe lexical se conjugue avec l'auxiliaire **do.**

⚠ À la forme affirmative, le verbe prend un ***s*** à la troisième personne du singulier, ou ***-es*** si le verbe se termine par ***-s***, ***-x***, ***-sh***, ***-ch*** ou ***-o*** :
→ *kiss-kisses, go-goes*

• Aux formes interrogative et négative, ***do*** devient ***does*** et ***don't*** devient ***doesn't*** à la troisième personne du singulier. À ces formes, c'est donc ***do*** et non la base verbale qui porte le ***-s*** à la troisième personne du singulier.

Forme affirmative	Forme interrogative	Forme négative	Réponse courte
He plays football on Saturdays.	***Does** he **play** football?*	*He **doesn't play** football.*	*Yes, he **does**. No, he **doesn't**.*
*I/you/we/they **play** football on Sundays.*	***Do** I/you/we/they **play** football?*	*I/you/we/they **don't play** football.*	*Yes, I/you/we /they **do**.* *No, I/you/we /they **don't**.*
*He **plays** football on Saturdays.*	***Does** he **play** football ?*	*He **doesn't play** football.*	*Yes, he **does**. No, he **doesn't**.*

17 Le présent en *be + V-ing*

• Tu utilises le présent en ***be*** + ***V-ing*** pour parler des **actions en cours.** Compare :
→ *–What does your father do?*
– He works in a bank.

• présent simple = caractéristique
→ *– And what is he doing?*
– I think he's having lunch.

• présent en *be* + *-ing* = action en cours

• Avec le present en ***be*** +***V-ing***, la personne qui parle utilise cette forme pour faire passer un autre message.
→ *Take your umbrella! It'**s raining**.* (conseil)
→ *Sorry, I can't come, I'**m having** lunch.* (excuse)

18 Le prétérit

- Tu utilises le **prétérit** pour parler du **passé.**

Be au prétérit

- ***Be*** a deux formes passées :

I, he, she, it	*We, you, they*
was	*were*

- Lorsque **be** est le verbe de la phrase, il se conjugue ainsi :

Forme affirmative	Forme interrogative	Forme négative
He was very tired.	*Were you tired?*	*They were not tired.*

Le prétérit des verbes lexicaux

- **La forme affirmative du prétérit**

La forme passée des verbes est **invariable**. Elle se forme ainsi :

Verbe dont la base finit par une consonne	Verbe dont la base finit par *-e*	Verbe irrégulier → voir liste ci-dessous
On ajoute ***-ed*** à la base verbale *finished – played – acted – watched...*	On ajoute **-d** à la base verbale *lived – arrived – danced...*	La forme passée doit être sue **par cœur** *made – met – took – slept...*

- **Les formes interrogative et négative du prétérit**

Aux formes **interrogative** et **négative**, le verbe lexical (tous les verbes autres que ***be***) se conjugue avec l'auxiliaire ***did*** à toutes les personnes. Le verbe apparaît donc sous sa forme de base verbale précédé de ***did***.

Forme affirmative	Forme interrogative	Forme négative	Réponse courte
*He danc**ed** a lot last night.* *He **had** a good holiday.*	***Did** he dance last night?* ***Did** you have a good holiday?*	*He **didn't** dance last night.* *He **didn't** have a good holiday.*	*Yes, he **did**.* *No, he **didn't**.*

Les verbes irréguliers			
be → was/were	do → did	have → had	run → ran
buy → bought	drink → drank	leave → left	see → saw
come → came	eat → ate	meet → met	swim → swam
cost → cost	go → went	make → made	take → took

19 Ago

- Tu utilises ***ago*** pour exprimer une durée.
- ***Ago*** est l'équivalent de "il y a". Il est toujours précédé d'une indication de durée et se place après l'expression de la durée.
  - → *He went to England five years **ago**.*
  - → *They discovered America six centuries **ago**.*

20 L'expression du futur

- ***will*** (voir Les auxiliaires de modalité p.165)
- ***be going to***

Tu utilises la forme ***be going to*** suivie de la base verbale pour parler de **tes intentions** ou **de ce qui va se passer à coup sûr selon toi**.
  - → ***I'm going to** call my grand-mother.*
  - → *I think it **is going to** rain.*
  - → *I'm sure **we're going to** win.*

21 Les auxiliaires de modalité

- Tu utilises les auxiliaires ***can***, ***must***, ***will*** ou ***should*** pour exprimer un **avis sur un événement**. Ils te permettent de dire si selon toi **un événement est possible**, **obligatoire**, **conseillé**…
- Chacun d'eux exprime une notion différente mais ils fonctionnent de la même façon :

→ aux formes affirmative et négative, ils se placent **entre le sujet et le verbe** ;
→ ils sont tous **invariables** ;
→ ils sont **suivis de la base verbale**.

À la forme négative, ils sont suivis de ***not***. Leurs formes contractées sont : ***can't***, ***mustn't***, ***won't***, ***shouldn't***.

	Forme affirmative	Forme interrogative	Forme négative
can	Capacité physique ou intellectuelle *She **can sing** very well.* Permission *You **can open** the window.*	***Can** she **dance** very well?*	Incapacité physique ou intellectuelle *She **can't dance** very well.* Interdiction *You **can't go**!*
should	Conseil *Your hair is too long, you **should go** to the hairdresser's.*		Conseil *You **shouldn't annoy** your little sister all the time.*
must	Obligation *You **must do** your homework.*	***Must** they **practise** every night?*	Interdiction *You **mustn't talk back** to your teachers.*
will	Volonté / certitude *I think I'**ll call** her this evening.* Expression du futur *When I'm 18, I **will travel** around the world.*	***Will** you **call** me this evening?*	Volonté / certitude *She **won't agree** with this idea.*

- ***Would***

Tu utilises ***would*** suivi de **like** ou **prefer** pour formuler **une demande** ou exprimer **une préférence**.

→ *I'd like some chocolate cake, please.*
→ *I would prefer to visit a castle.*

22 Les adverbes de fréquence

Tu utilises les adverbes de fréquence pour **dire à quelle fréquence (tous les combien) un événement se produit**.

never	rarely	sometimes	often	always
jamais	rarement	parfois	souvent	toujours

Les adverbes de fréquence se placent devant le verbe, mais toujours après ***be***.

Forme affirmative	Forme interrogative	Forme négative
***He often plays** the guitar at night.* ***We're always** late for school!*	***Does he often play** the guitar?* ***Are you often** late for school?*	***We don't often have** parties.* ***She's always** on time.*

⚠ Les expressions qui expriment une fréquence se placent en début ou en fin de phrase.
→ *He goes to the drama club **every day** / **once a week** / **twice a week**…*

Lexique anglais-français

Ce lexique permet de comprendre tous les contenus du manuel.

Abréviations utilisées

adj. : adjectif	**conj.** : conjonction	**n.** : nom	**pron.** : pronom	**v. irrég.** : verbe irrégulier
adv. : adverbe	**excl.** : exclamation	**prép.** : préposition	**v.** : verbe	**onomat.** : onomatopée

A

abbey	*(n.)*	['æbɪ]	*abbaye*
about	*(adv.)*	[ə'baʊt]	*à propos de, environ*
accept	*(v.)*	[ək'sept]	*accepter*
act	*(v.)*	[ækt]	*interpréter*
actor	*(n.)*	['æktəʳ]	*acteur*
actress	*(n.)*	['æktrəs]	*actrice*
adjective	*(n.)*	['ædzektɪv]	*adjectif*
admire	*(v.)*	[əd'maɪəʳ]	*admirer*
admiring	*(adj.)*	[əd'maɪərɪŋ]	*admiratif*
afternoon	*(n.)*	[ˌɑːftə'nuːn]	*après-midi*
aggressive	*(adj.)*	[ə'gresɪv]	*agressif*
airport	*(n.)*	['ɛəpɔːt]	*aéroport*
also	*(adv.)*	['ɔːlsəʊ]	*aussi*
always	*(adv.)*	['ɔːlweɪz]	*toujours*
amazing	*(adj.)*	[ə'meɪzɪŋ]	*surprenant, stupéfiant*
American	*(adj.)*	[ə'merɪkən]	*américain*
angry	*(adj.)*	['æŋgrɪ]	*en colère*
answer	*(v.)*	['ɑːnsəʳ]	*répondre*
anyway	*(adv.)*	['enɪweɪ]	*de toute façon*
apple	*(n.)*	['æpl]	*pomme*
April	*(n.)*	['eɪprəl]	*avril*
archery	*(n.)*	['ɑːtərɪ]	*tir à l'arc*
arm	*(n.)*	[ɑːm]	*bras*
armour	*(n.)*	['ɑːməʳ]	*armure*
arrive	*(v.)*	[ə'raɪv]	*arriver*
arrow	*(n.)*	['ærəʊ]	*flèche*
art	*(n.)*	[ɑːt]	*arts plastiques*
article	*(n.)*	['ɑːtɪkl]	*article*
at	*(prép.)*	[æt]	*à*
athletic	*(adj.)*	[æθ'letɪk]	*sportif*
attractive	*(adj.)*	[ə'træktɪv]	*séduisant*
audience	*(n.)*	['ɔːdɪəns]	*public*
audition	*(v.)*	[ɔː'dɪfən]	*passer un casting*
audition	*(n.)*	[ɔː'dɪfən]	*casting / audition*
August	*(n.)*	['ɔːgəst]	*août*
aunt	*(n.)*	[ɑːnt]	*tante*
Australian	*(adj.)*	[ɒ'streɪlɪən]	*australien*
autumn	*(n.)*	['ɔːtəm]	*automne*

B

bacon	*(n.)*	['beɪkən]	*bacon*
bad	*(adj.)*	[bæd]	*mauvais*
bake	*(v.)*	[beɪk]	*cuire au four*
bakery	*(n.)*	['beɪkərɪ]	*boulangerie*
basket	*(n.)*	['bɑːskɪt]	*panier*
bat	*(n.)*	[bæt]	*chauve souris*
bathroom	*(n.)*	['bɑːθrʊm]	*salle de bain*
be	*(v. irrég.)*	[biː]	*être*
be afraid	*(v. irrég.)*	[biː 'əfreɪd]	*avoir peur*
be born	*(v. irrég.)*	[biː bɔːn]	*naître*
beans	*(n.)*	[biːns]	*haricots*
bear	*(n.)*	[bɛəʳ]	*ours*
beat	*(v. irrég.)*	[biːt]	*battre*
beautiful	*(adj.)*	['bjuːtɪfʊl]	*beau*
because	*(conj.)*	[bɪ'kɒz]	*parce que*
become	*(v. irrég.)*	[bɪ'kʌm]	*devenir*
bed	*(n.)*	[bed]	*lit*
bedroom	*(n.)*	['bedrʊm]	*chambre*
beef	*(n.)*	[biːf]	*bœuf*
begin	*(v. irrég.)*	[bɪ'gɪn]	*commencer*
behind	*(prép.)*	[bɪ'haɪnd]	*derrière*
best	*(adj.)*	[best]	*meilleur*
better	*(adj.)*	['betəʳ]	*mieux / meilleur*
between	*(prép.)*	[bɪ'twiːn]	*entre*
bike	*(n.)*	[baɪk]	*vélo*
bin	*(n.)*	[bɪn]	*poubelle*
biology	*(n.)*	[baɪ'ɒlədʒɪ]	*biologie*
bird	*(n.)*	[bɜːd]	*oiseau*
birthday	*(n.)*	['bɜːθdeɪ]	*anniversaire*
biscuit	*(n.)*	['bɪskɪt]	*biscuit*
black	*(adj.)*	[blæk]	*noir*
blue	*(adj.)*	[bluː]	*bleu*
board	*(n.)*	[bɔːd]	*tableau*
boat	*(n.)*	[bəʊt]	*bateau*
book	*(n.)*	[bʊk]	*livre*
bookshop	*(n.)*	['bʊkʃɒːp]	*librairie*
box	*(n.)*	[bɒks]	*boîte*
brave	*(adj.)*	[breɪv]	*courageux*
bread	*(n.)*	[bred]	*pain*
break	*(v. irrég.)*	[breɪk]	*casser*
break	*(n.)*	[breɪk]	*pause*
breakfast	*(n.)*	['brekfəst]	*petit déjeuner*
bring	*(v. irrég.)*	[brɪŋ]	*apporter*
British	*(adj.)*	['brɪtɪʃ]	*britannique*
broom	*(n.)*	[brʊm]	*balai*
brother	*(n.)*	['brʌðəʳ]	*frère*
brown	*(adj.)*	[braʊn]	*marron*
buddy	*(n.)*	['bʌdɪ]	*copain*
build	*(v. irrég.)*	[bɪld]	*construire*
building	*(n.)*	['bɪldɪŋ]	*bâtiment*
but	*(conj.)*	[bʌt]	*mais / sauf*
buy	*(v. irrég.)*	[baɪ]	*acheter*
by	*(prép.)*	[baɪ]	*par*

C

catch	*(v. irrég.)*	[kætʃ]	*attraper*
cafeteria	*(n.)*	[kæʃɪ'tɪərɪə]	*cantine, cafétéria*
cake	*(n.)*	[keɪk]	*gâteau*
calendar	*(n.)*	['kæləndəʳ]	*calendrier*
call	*(n.)*	[kɔːl]	*appel*
call	*(v.)*	[kɔːl]	*appeler*
can	*(v.)*	[kæn]	*pouvoir / savoir faire*
candy bars	*(n.)*	['kændɪ baːʳz]	*bonbons*
cap	*(n.)*	[kæp]	*casquette*
car	*(n.)*	[kaːʳ]	*voiture*
careful	*(adj.)*	['kɛəfʊl]	*attentionné*
carrot	*(n.)*	['kærət]	*carotte*
cartoon	*(n.)*	[kɑː'tuːn]	*dessin animé*
castle	*(n.)*	['kɑːsl]	*château*
cat	*(n.)*	[kæt]	*chat*
catch	*(v. irrég.)*	[kætʃ]	*attraper*
cathedral	*(n.)*	[kə'θiːdrəl]	*cathédrale*
celebrations	*(n.)*	['selɪ'breɪʃənz]	*festivités*
cell phone	*(n.)*	['selfəʊn]	*téléphone mobile*
chair	*(n.)*	[tʃɛəʳ]	*chaise*
challenge	*(v.)*	['tʃælɪndz]	*défier*

character	*(n.)*	['kærɪktəʳ]	*personnage*
chat	*(v.)*	[tʃæt]	*bavarder*
cheap	*(adj.)*	[tʃi:p]	*bon marché*
cheer	*(v.)*	[tʃɪəʳ]	*acclamer*
cheerful	*(adj.)*	[tʃɪəful]	*joyeux, gai*
cheese	*(n.)*	[tʃi:z]	*fromage*
chicken	*(n.)*	['tʃɪkɪn]	*poulet*
child	*(n.)*	[tʃaɪld]	*enfant*
children	*(n.)*	['tʃɪldrən]	*enfants*
chips	*(n.)*	[tʃɪps]	*frites*
chocolate	*(n.)*	['tʃɒklɪt]	*chocolat*
choose	*(v. irrég.)*	[tʃu:z]	*choisir*
Christmas	*(n.)*	['krɪsməs]	*Noël*
church	*(n.)*	[tʃɜ:tʃ]	*église*
city	*(n.)*	['sɪtɪ]	*ville*
class rules	*(n.)*	['klɑ:s ru:lz]	*règlement de classe*
classmate	*(n.)*	['klɑ:smeɪt]	*camarade*
classroom	*(n.)*	['klɑ:srʊm]	*salle de classe*
clever	*(adj.)*	['klevəʳ]	*intelligent*
clock	*(n.)*	[klɒk]	*horloge*
close	*(adv.)*	[kləʊs]	*proche de*
close	*(v.)*	[kləʊz]	*fermer*
clothes	*(n.)*	[kləʊsðz]	*habits*
cloudy	*(n.)*	[klaʊdɪ]	*nuageux*
clue	*(n.)*	[klu:]	*indice*
clumsy	*(adj.)*	['klʌmzɪ]	*maladroit*
coach	*(n.)*	[kəʊtʃ]	*entraîneur*
coat	*(n.)*	[kəʊt]	*manteau*
Coke	*(n.)*	[kəʊk]	*coca*
colour	*(n.)*	['kʌləʳ]	*couleur*
come	*(v. irrég.)*	[kʌm]	*venir*
comfortable	*(adj.)*	['kʌmfətəbl]	*comfortable*
computer	*(n.)*	[kəm'pju:təʳ]	*ordinateur*
concert	*(n.)*	['kɒnsət]	*concert*
confident	*(adj.)*	['kɒnfɪdənt]	*confiant*
congratulate	*(v.)*	[kən,grætjʊleɪt]	*féliciter*
congratulations	*(n.)*	[kən,græt jʊ'leɪʃənz]	*félicitations*
cook	*(v.)*	[kʊk]	*faire à manger*
cool	*(adj.)*	[ku:l]	*sympathique*
copybook	*(n.)*	['kɒpɪbʊk]	*cahier*
costume	*(n.)*	['kɒstju:m]	*costume (de théatre)*
country	*(n.)*	['kʌntrɪ]	*pays*
cousin	*(n.)*	['kʌzn]	*cousin, cousine*
crazy	*(adj.)*	['kreɪzɪ]	*fou*
crisps	*(n.)*	[krɪsps]	*chips*
cross	*(adj.)*	[krɒs]	*en colère*
crown	*(n.)*	[kraʊn]	*couronne*
cry	*(v.)*	[kraɪ]	*pleurer*
curtain	*(n.)*	['kɜ:tn]	*rideau*
customer	*(n.)*	['kʌstəməʳ]	*client*
cycling	*(n.)*	['saɪklɪŋ]	*cyclisme*

D

dance	*(v.)*	[dɑ:ns]	*danser*
dancer	*(n.)*	['dɑ:nsəʳ]	*danseur*
dangerous	*(adj.)*	['deɪndʒrəs]	*dangereux*
dark	*(adj.)*	[dɑ:k]	*sombre*
daughter	*(n.)*	['dɔ:təʳ]	*fille*
day	*(n.)*	[deɪ]	*jour, journée*
December	*(n.)*	[dɪ'sembəʳ]	*décembre*
decide	*(v.)*	[dɪ'saɪd]	*décider*
defeat	*(n.)*	[dɪ'fi:t]	*défaite*
delicious	*(adj.)*	[dɪ'lɪʃəs]	*délicieux*
desk	*(n.)*	[desk]	*bureau (meuble)*
dessert	*(n.)*	[dɪ'zɜ:t]	*dessert*
difficult	*(adj.)*	['dɪfɪkəlt]	*difficile*
dining-room	*(n.)*	['daɪnɪŋ ,rʊm]	*salle à manger*
dinner	*(n.)*	['dɪnəʳ]	*repas du soir*
dip	*(v.)*	['dɪp]	*tremper*
discover	*(v.)*	[dɪs'kʌvəʳ]	*découvrir*
discuss	*(v.)*	[dɪs'kʌs]	*discuter*
disappointed	*(adj.)*	[,dɪsə'pɔɪntɪd]	*déçu*
do	*(v. irrég.)*	[du:]	*faire*
doctor	*(n.)*	['dɒktəʳ]	*docteur*
dog	*(n.)*	[dɒg]	*chien*
door	*(n.)*	[dɔ:ʳ]	*porte*
downstairs	*(adv.)*	['daʊn'steəz]	*en bas*
dozen	*(adj.)*	['dʌzn]	*douzaine*
draw	*(v. irrég.)*	[drɔ:]	*dessiner*
dream	*(v. irrég.)*	[dri:m]	*rêver*
dress	*(n.)*	[dres]	*robe*
dress up	*(v.)*	[dres ʌp]	*déguiser (se)*
drink	*(v. irrég.)*	[drɪŋk]	*boire*
drive	*(v. irrég.)*	[draɪv]	*conduire*
dungeon	*(n.)*	['dʌndʒən]	*cachot/donjon*
during	*(adv.)*	['djʊərɪŋ]	*pendant*

E

ear	*(n.)*	[ɪəʳ]	*oreille*
easy	*(adj.)*	['i:zɪ]	*facile*
eat	*(v. irrég.)*	[i:t]	*manger*
egg	*(n.)*	[eg]	*œuf*
embarrassed	*(adj.)*	[ɪm'bærəst]	*embarrassé, gêné*
emotional	*(adj.)*	[ɪ'məʊʃənl]	*émouvant*
enemy	*(n.)*	['enəmɪ]	*ennemi*
English	*(adj.)*	['ɪŋglɪʃ]	*anglais*
eraser	*(n.)*	[ɪ'reɪzr]	*gomme*
evening	*(n.)*	['i:vnɪŋ]	*soir*
every	*(adj.)*	['evrɪ]	*chaque*
everybody	*(pron.)*	['evrɪbɒdɪ]	*tout le monde*
everywhere	*(adv.)*	['evrɪweəʳ]	*partout*
excited	*(adj.)*	[ɪk'saɪtɪd]	*enthousiaste*
exercise	*(v.)*	['eksəsaɪz]	*faire du sport*
exercise	*(n.)*	['eksəsaɪz]	*exercice*
exist	*(v.)*	[ɪg'zɪst]	*exister*
expensive	*(adj.)*	[ek'spensɪv]	*cher*
explain	*(v.)*	[ek'spleɪn]	*expliquer*
explore	*(v.)*	[ek'splɔ:ʳ]	*explorer*
eye	*(n.)*	[aɪ]	*œil*

F

face	*(n.)*	[feɪs]	*visage*
fall	*(v. irrég.)*	[fɔ:l]	*tomber*
false	*(adj.)*	[fɔ:ls]	*faux*
family	*(n.)*	['fæmɪlɪ]	*famille*
family tree	*(n.)*	['fæmɪlɪ tri:]	*arbre généalogique*
famous	*(adj.)*	['feɪməs]	*célèbre*
farm	*(n.)*	[fɑ:m]	*ferme*
fashion	*(n.)*	['fæʃən]	*mode*
fashion show	*(n.)*	['fæʃən ʃəʊ]	*défilé de mode*
fast	*(adj.)*	[fɑ:st]	*rapide*
father	*(n.)*	['fɑ:ðəʳ]	*père*
favourite	*(adj.)*	['feɪvərɪt]	*préféré*
February	*(n.)*	['febrʊərɪ]	*février*
feel	*(v. irrég.)*	[fi:l]	*sentir (se)*
feeling	*(n.)*	['fi:lɪŋ]	*sentiment*
fight	*(v. irrég.)*	[faɪt]	*combattre*
film	*(n.)*	[fɪlm]	*film*
film director	*(n.)*	[fɪlm dɪ'rektəʳ]	*metteur en scène*
find	*(v. irrég.)*	[faɪnd]	*trouver*
fine	*(adj.)*	[faɪn]	*en forme*
finger	*(n.)*	['fɪŋgəʳ]	*doigt*
fireplace	*(n.)*	['faɪəpleɪs]	*cheminée*
first	*(adv.)*	[fɜ:st]	*premier*
fish	*(n.)*	[fɪʃ]	*poisson*
floor	*(n.)*	[flɔ:ʳ]	*sol*
flower	*(n.)*	['flaʊəʳ]	*fleur*

Lexique anglais-français

fly	*(v. irrég.)*	[flaɪ]	*voler*
follow	*(v.)*	['fɒləʊ]	*suivre*
food	*(n.)*	[fuːd]	*nourriture*
football	*(n.)*	['fʊtbɔːl]	*football / ballon de foot*
forest	*(n.)*	['fɒrɪst]	*forêt*
forget	*(v. irrég.)*	[fə'get]	*oublier*
fortunately	*(adv.)*	['fɔːtʃənɪtlɪ]	*heureusement*
found	*(v.)*	[faʊnd]	*fonder*
free	*(adj.)*	[friː]	*libre / gratuit*
French	*(adj.)*	[frentʃ]	*français*
Friday	*(n.)*	['fraɪdeɪ]	*vendredi*
friend	*(n.)*	[frend]	*ami*
fruit	*(n.)*	[fruːt]	*fruits*
fruit juice	*(n.)*	[fruːt dzuːs]	*jus de fruits*
funny	*(adj.)*	['fʌnɪ]	*drôle*
furious	*(adj.)*	['fjʊərɪəs]	*furieux*
furniture	*(n.)*	['fɜːnɪtʃə^{r}]	*meubles*

G

game	*(n.)*	[geɪm]	*jeu*
garden	*(n.)*	['gɑːdn]	*jardin*
geography	*(n.)*	[dʒɪ'ɒgrəfɪ]	*géographie*
get dressed	*(v. irrég.)*	[get drest]	*habiller (s')*
get ready	*(v. irrég.)*	[get 'redɪ]	*préparer (se)*
get up	*(v. irrég.)*	[get ʌp]	*se lever*
ghost	*(n.)*	[gəʊst]	*fantôme*
give	*(v. irrég.)*	[gɪv]	*donner*
glasses	*(n.)*	[glɑːsɪz]	*lunettes*
glue stick	*(n.)*	[gluː stɪk]	*colle*
go	*(v. irrég.)*	[gəʊ]	*aller*
go back	*(v. irrég.)*	[gəʊ bæk]	*retourner*
go straight	*(v. irrég.)*	[gəʊ streɪt]	*aller tout droit*
goal	*(n.)*	[gəʊl]	*but*
good	*(adj.)*	[gʊd]	*bon*
good afternoon	*(excl.)*	[gʊd 'ɑːftə'nuvn]	*bonjour (l'après-midi)*
good evening	*(excl.)*	[gʊd 'iːvnɪŋ]	*bonsoir*
good morning	*(excl.)*	[gʊd 'mɔːnɪŋ]	*bonjour (le matin)*
good night	*(excl.)*	[gʊd 'naɪt]	*bonne nuit*
goodbye	*(excl.)*	[gʊd'baɪ]	*au revoir*
good-looking	*(adj.)*	[gʊd 'lʊkɪŋ]	*beau*
gorilla	*(n.)*	[gə'rɪlə]	*gorille*
granddaughter	*(n.)*	['grændɔːtə^{r}]	*petite-fille*
grandfather	*(n.)*	['grændfɑːðə^{r}]	*grand-père*
grandma	*(n.)*	['grændmɑː]	*grand-mère*
grandmother	*(n.)*	['grænmʌðə^{r}]	*grand-mère*
grandson	*(n.)*	['grænsʌn]	*petit-fils*
grass	*(n.)*	[grɑːs]	*herbe*
great	*(adj.)*	[greɪt]	*grand / super*
green	*(adj.)*	[griːn]	*vert*
greetings	*(n.)*	[greɪtɪŋz]	*salutations*
grey	*(adj.)*	[greɪ]	*gris*
guard	*(n.)*	[gɑːd]	*garde*
guess	*(v.)*	[ges]	*deviner*
guitar	*(n.)*	[gɪ'tɑː^{r}]	*guitare*

H

hair	*(n.)*	[hɛə^{r}]	*cheveux*
hall	*(n.)*	[hɔːl]	*couloir, hall d'entrée*
ham	*(n.)*	[hæm]	*jambon*
hamster	*(n.)*	['hæmstə^{r}]	*hamster*
happy	*(adj.)*	['hæpɪ]	*content*
hard	*(adj.)*	[hɑːd]	*difficile*
hard-working	*(adj.)*	[hɑːd 'wɜːkɪŋ]	*travailleur*
hat	*(n.)*	[hæt]	*chapeau*
hate	*(v.)*	[heɪt]	*détester*
have	*(v. irrég.)*	[hæv]	*avoir*
have fun	*(v. irrég.)*	[hæv fʌn]	*amuser (s')*
head	*(n.)*	[hed]	*tête*
headmaster	*(n.)*	['hedmɑːstə^{r}]	*principal*
healthy	*(adj.)*	['helθɪ]	*bon pour la santé*
hear	*(v. irrég.)*	[hɪə^{r}]	*entendre*
heart	*(n.)*	[hɑːt]	*cœur*
hello	*(excl.)*	[hə'ləʊ]	*bonjour*
help	*(v.)*	[help]	*aider*
hero	*(n.)*	['hɪərəʊ]	*héros*
hi!	*(interj.)*	[haɪ]	*salut*
hide	*(v. irrég.)*	[haɪd]	*cacher (se)*
high	*(adj.)*	[haɪ]	*haut*
history	*(n.)*	['hɪstərɪ]	*histoire*
hit	*(v. irrég.)*	[hɪt]	*frapper*
hobbies	*(n.)*	['hɒbɪz]	*passe-temps*
holiday	*(n.)*	['hɒlɪdeɪ]	*vacances, jour férié*
home	*(n.)*	[həʊm]	*maison, chez-soi*
homework	*(n.)*	['həʊmwɜːk]	*devoirs*
honey	*(n.)*	['hʌnɪ]	*miel*
hospital	*(n.)*	['hɒspɪtl]	*hôpital*
hostile	*(adj.)*	['hɒstaɪl]	*hostile*
hotel	*(n.)*	[həʊ'tel]	*hôtel*
house	*(n.)*	[haʊs]	*maison*
how	*(pron.)*	[haʊ]	*comment*
how many	*(pron.)*	[haʊ 'menɪ]	*combien (+ nom pluriel)*
how much	*(pron.)*	[haʊ mʌtʃ]	*combien (+ nom singulier)*
how old	*(pron.)*	[haʊ əʊld]	*quel âge*
hungry	*(adj.)*	['hʌŋgrɪ]	*(be hungry) avoir faim*
hurry up	*(v.)*	['hʌrɪ ʌp]	*se dépêcher*
hurt	*(v. irrég.)*	[hɜːt]	*faire mal*

I

ice cream	*(n.)*	[aɪs kriːm]	*glace (à manger)*
idea	*(n.)*	[aɪ'dɪə]	*idée*
identity	*(n.)*	[aɪ'dentɪtɪ]	*identité*
illustrate	*(v.)*	['ɪləstreɪt]	*illustrer*
impressed	*(adj.)*	[ɪm'prest]	*impressionné*
impressive	*(adj.)*	[ɪm'presɪv]	*impressionnant*
in	*(prép.)*	[ɪn]	*dans, à*
in front of	*(prép.)*	[ɪn frʌnt ɒv]	*devant*
include	*(v.)*	[ɪn'kluːd]	*inclure*
incredible	*(adj.)*	[ɪn'kredəbl]	*incroyable*
infirmary	*(n.)*	[ɪn'fɜːmərɪ]	*infirmerie*
inside	*(prép.)*	['ɪn'saɪd]	*à l'intérieur*
interested	*(adj.)*	['ɪntrɪstɪd]	*intéressé*
interesting	*(adj.)*	['ɪntrɪstɪŋ]	*intéressant*
introduce	*(v.)*	[ˌɪntrə'djuːs]	*présenter*
invent	*(v.)*	[ɪn'vent]	*inventer*
Irish	*(adj.)*	['aɪərɪʃ]	*irlandais*
itinerary	*(n.)*	[aɪ'tɪnərərɪ]	*itinéraire*

J

jacket	*(n.)*	['dʒækɪt]	*veste*
January	*(n.)*	['dʒænjʊərɪ]	*janvier*
jar	*(n.)*	['dʒɑː^{r}]	*pot*
jelly	*(n.)*	['dʒelɪ]	*gelée*
jewel	*(n.)*	['dʒuːəl]	*bijoux*
joke	*(n.)*	[dʒəʊk]	*blague*
July	*(n.)*	[dʒuː'laɪ]	*juillet*
jump	*(v.)*	[dʒʌmp]	*sauter*
jumper	*(n.)*	['dʒʌmpə^{r}]	*pull-over*
June	*(n.)*	[dʒuːn]	*juin*

K

key	*(n.)*	[kiː]	*clé*
key ring	*(n.)*	[kiːtʃeɪn]	*porte-clés*
kick	*(v.)*	[kɪk]	*donner un coup de pied*
king	*(n.)*	[kɪŋ]	*roi*
kiss	*(v.)*	[kɪs]	*embrasser*
kitchen	*(n.)*	['kɪtʃɪn]	*cuisine*
kitten	*(n.)*	['kɪtn]	*chaton*
knee	*(n.)*	[niː]	*genou*
knight	*(n.)*	[naɪt]	*chevalier*
know	*(v. irrég.)*	[nəʊ]	*savoir / connaître*

L

lady	*(n.)*	['leɪdɪ]	*dame*
lamp	*(n.)*	[læmp]	*lampe*
last	*(adj.)*	[lɑːst]	*dernier*
late	*(adv.)*	[leɪt]	*en retard*
learn	*(v. irrég.)*	[lɜːn]	*apprendre*
left	*(adv.)*	[left]	*à gauche*
leg	*(n.)*	[leg]	*jambe*
lesson	*(n.)*	['lesn]	*leçon*
life	*(n.)*	[laɪf]	*vie*
life habits	*(n.)*	[laɪf 'hæbɪt]	*habitudes de vie*
lifestyle	*(n.)*	[laɪfstaɪl]	*style de vie*
like	*(conj.)*	[laɪk]	*comme*
like	*(v.)*	[laɪk]	*aimer (bien)*
lip	*(n.)*	[lɪp]	*lèvre*
listen (to)	*(v.)*	['lɪsn]	*écouter*
live	*(v.)*	[lɑiv]	*habiter*
live	*(adj.)*	['lɪv]	*(en) direct*
living-room	*(n.)*	['lɪvɪŋ rʊm]	*salon*
look	*(v.)*	[lʊk]	*regarder*
lose	*(v. irrég.)*	[luːz]	*perdre*
lots of	*(adv.)*	[lɒts ɒv]	*beaucoup de*
love	*(v.)*	[lʌv]	*aimer*
lucky	*(adj.)*	['lʌkɪ]	*chanceux*
lunch	*(n.)*	[lʌntʃ]	*repas du midi*

M

mad	*(adj.)*	[mæd]	*fou, en colère*
main	*(adj.)*	[meɪn]	*principal*
make	*(v. irrég.)*	[meɪk]	*faire*
map	*(n.)*	[mæp]	*carte*
March	*(n.)*	[mɑːtʃ]	*mars*
maths	*(n.)*	[mæθs]	*mathématiques*
May	*(n.)*	[meɪ]	*mai*
meal	*(n.)*	[miːl]	*repas*
mean	*(v. irrég.)*	[miːn]	*vouloir dire, signifier*
meat	*(n.)*	[miːt]	*viande*
meet	*(v. irrég.)*	[miːt]	*rencontrer (se)*
merry	*(adj.)*	['merɪ]	*joyeux*
mess	*(n.)*	[mes]	*bazar, désordre*
midnight	*(adv.)*	['mɪdnaɪt]	*minuit*
milk	*(n.)*	[mɪlk]	*lait*
miss	*(v.)*	[mɪs]	*manquer*
miss	*(n.)*	[mɪs]	*mademoiselle*
Monday	*(n.)*	['mʌndeɪ]	*lundi*
monster	*(n.)*	['mɒnstəʳ]	*monstre*
month	*(n.)*	[mʌnθ]	*mois*
more	*(adv.)*	[mɔːʳ]	*plus*
morning	*(n.)*	['mɔːnɪŋ]	*matin*
mother	*(n.)*	['mʌðəʳ]	*mère*
mouse	*(n.)*	[maʊs]	*souris*
mouth	*(n.)*	[maʊθ]	*bouche*
move	*(v.)*	[muːv]	*bouger*
move to one side	*(v.)*	[muːv]	*se décaler*
mug	*(n.)*	[mʌg]	*grande tasse*
museum	*(n.)*	[mjuː'zɪəm]	*musée*
musical	*(n.)*	['mjuː'zɪkəl]	*comédie musicale*
must	*(v.)*	[mʌst]	*devoir*

N

name	*(n.)*	[neɪm]	*nom*
nationality	*(n.)*	[ˌnæʃə'nælɪtɪ]	*nationalité*
near	*(prép.)*	[nɪəʳ]	*près de*
nervous	*(adj.)*	['nɜːvəs]	*nerveux*
never	*(adv.)*	['nevəʳ]	*jouer*
next	*(adj.)*	[nekst]	*prochain*
next to	*(prép.)*	[nekst tuː]	*à côté de*
nice	*(adj.)*	[naɪs]	*joli, agréable*
night	*(n.)*	[naɪt]	*nuit*
nightmare	*(n.)*	['naɪtmɛəʳ]	*cauchemar*
nose	*(n.)*	[nəʊz]	*nez*
nothing	*(adv.)*	['nʌθɪŋ]	*rien*
noun	*(n.)*	[naʊn]	*nom (commun)*
November	*(n.)*	[nəʊ'vembəʳ]	*novembre*

O

October	*(n.)*	[ɒk'təʊbəʳ]	*octobre*
often	*(adv.)*	['ɒfən]	*souvent*
old	*(adj.)*	[əʊld]	*vieux, âgé*
on	*(prép.)*	[ɒn]	*sur*
on tiptoe	*(adv.)*	[ɒn 'tɪptəʊ]	*sur la pointe des pieds*
only	*(adv.)*	['əʊnlɪ]	*seulement*
open	*(v.)*	['əʊpən]	*ouvrir*
orange juice	*(n.)*	['ɒrɪndʒ dʒuːs]	*jus d'orange*
organic food	*(n.)*	['ɔːggænɪk fuːd]	*nourriture bio*
organize	*(v.)*	['ɔːgənaɪz]	*organiser*
other	*(adj.)*	['ʌðəʳ]	*autre*
ouch!	*(onomat.)*	[aʊtʃ]	*aïe !*
outside	*(prép.).*	['aʊt'saɪd]	*à l'extérieur*

P

P.E.	*(n.)*	[piː'iː]	*éducation physique*
painting	*(n.)*	['peɪntɪŋ]	*tableau*
pal	*(n.)*	[pæl]	*copain*
parent	*(n.)*	['pɛərənt]	*parent*
park	*(n.)*	[pɑːk]	*parc*
part	*(n.)*	[pɑːt]	*partie / rôle*
party	*(n.)*	['pɑːtɪ]	*fête*
past	*(n.)*	[pɑːst]	*passé*
pen	*(n.)*	[pen]	*stylo*
pen friend	*(n.)*	[pen frend]	*correspondant*
pencil	*(n.)*	['pensl]	*crayon*
pencil case	*(n.)*	['pensl keɪs]	*trousse*
pencil sharpener	*(n.)*	['pensl 'fɑːpnəʳ]	*taille-crayon*
perfect	*(adj.)*	['pɜːfɪkt]	*parfait*
performance	*(n.)*	[pə'fɔːməns]	*représentation*
person	*(n.)*	['pɜːsn]	*personne*
pet	*(n.)*	[pet]	*animal domestique*
phone	*(n.)*	[fəʊn]	*téléphone*
photographer	*(n.)*	[fə'tɒgrəfəʳ]	*photographe*
picture	*(n.)*	['pɪktʃəʳ]	*image*
pink	*(adj.)*	[pɪŋk]	*rose*
pitch	*(n.)*	[pɪtʃ]	*terrain*
place	*(n.)*	[pleɪs]	*lieu*
plate	*(n.)*	[pleɪt]	*assiette*
play	*(n.)*	[pleɪ]	*pièce de théatre*
play	*(v.)*	[pleɪ]	*jouer*
player	*(n.)*	['pleɪəʳ]	*joueur*
playground	*(n.)*	['pleɪgraʊnd]	*cour de récréation*
poor	*(adj.)*	[pʊəʳ]	*pauvre*
pork chop	*(n.)*	[pɔːk]	*côtelette de porc*
post office	*(n.)*	['pəʊstˌɒfɪs]	*poste*
potato	*(n.)*	[pə'teɪtəʊ]	*pomme de terre*

power	*(n.)*	['paʊəʳ]	*pouvoir*
precise	*(adj.)*	[prɪ'saɪs]	*précis*
prefer	*(v.)*	[prɪ'fɜːʳ]	*préférer*
prepare	*(v.)*	[prɪ'pɜəʳ]	*préparer (se)*
pretentious	*(adj.)*	[prɪ'tenʃəs]	*prétentieux*
pretty	*(adj.)*	['prɪtɪ]	*joli*
price	*(n.)*	[praɪs]	*prix*
problem	*(n.)*	['prɒbləm]	*problème*
proud	*(adj.)*	[praʊd]	*fier*
pub	*(n.)*	[pʌb]	*pub, café*
pupil	*(n.)*	['pjuːpl]	*élève*
put on	*(v. irrég.)*	[pʊt ɒn]	*enfiler*

Q

quality	*(n.)*	['kwɒlɪtɪ]	*qualité*
queen	*(n.)*	[kwiːn]	*reine*
queue	*(v.)*	[kjuː]	*faire la queue*
quick	*(adj.)*	['kwɪk]	*rapide*
quiet	*(adj.)*	['kwaɪət]	*calme*

R

rabbit	*(n.)*	['ræbɪt]	*lapin*
race	*(n.)*	[reɪs]	*course*
rain	*(n.)*	[reɪn]	*pluie*
rain	*(v.)*	[reɪn]	*pleuvoir*
raise	*(v.)*	[reɪz]	*lever*
rat	*(n.)*	[ræt]	*rat*
raven	*(n.)*	['reɪvn]	*corbeau*
read	*(v. irrég.)*	[riːd]	*lire*
ready	*(adj.)*	['redɪ]	*prêt*
really	*(adv.)*	['rɪəlɪ]	*vraiment*
recognize	*(v.)*	['rekəgnaɪz]	*reconnaître*
red	*(adj.)*	[red]	*rouge*
referee	*(n.)*	['refə'riː]	*arbitre*
registration	*(n.)*	['redzɪ'streɪʃən]	*appel*
remember	*(v.)*	[rɪ'membəʳ]	*souvenir (se)*
repeat	*(v.)*	[rɪ'piːt]	*répéter*
restaurant	*(n.)*	['restərɔːŋ]	*restaurant*
riddle	*(n.)*	['rɪdl]	*devinette*
right	*(adv.)*	[raɪt]	*à droite*
ring	*(n.)*	[rɪŋ]	*bague*
risk	*(v.)*	['rɪsk]	*risquer*
river	*(n.)*	['rɪvəʳ]	*rivière*
road	*(n.)*	[rəʊd]	*route*
role	*(n.)*	[rəʊl]	*rôle*
room	*(n.)*	[rʊm]	*pièce (maison)*
ruler	*(n.)*	['ruːləʳ]	*règle*
run	*(v. irrég.)*	[rʌn]	*courrir*

S

sad	*(adj.)*	[sæd]	*triste*
sail	*(v.)*	[seɪl]	*naviguer*
salad	*(n.)*	['sæləd]	*salade*
satisfy	*(v.)*	['sætɪsfaɪ]	*satisfaire*
Saturday	*(n.)*	['sætədeɪ]	*samedi*
sausages	*(n.)*	['sɒsɪdʒəz]	*saucisses*
say	*(v. irrég.)*	[seɪ]	*dire*
scared	*(adj.)*	[skɛəd]	*effrayé*
scary	*(adj.)*	['skɛərɪ]	*effrayant*
school	*(n.)*	[skuːl]	*école*
school bag	*(n.)*	[skuːl bæg]	*cartable*
school day	*(n.)*	[skuːl deɪ]	*jour d'école*
scissors	*(n.)*	['sɪzəz]	*ciseaux*
score	*(v.)*	[skɔːʳ]	*marquer*
Scottish	*(adj.)*	['skɒtɪʃ]	*écossais*
scream	*(v.)*	[skriːm]	*hurler*
sea	*(n.)*	[siː]	*mer*
season	*(n.)*	['siːzn]	*saison*
see	*(v. irrég.)*	[siː]	*voir*
sensitive	*(adj.)*	['sensɪtɪv]	*sensible*
sentence	*(n.)*	['sentəns]	*phrase*
sentimental	*(adj.)*	['sentɪ'mentl]	*sentimental*
September	*(n.)*	[sep'tembəʳ]	*septembre*
setting	*(n.)*	['setɪŋ]	*décor*
shadow	*(n.)*	['ʃædəʊ]	*ombre*
sheet	*(n.)*	[ʃiːt]	*feuille / drap*
shelf	*(n.)*	[ʃelf]	*étagère*
shine	*(v. irrég.)*	[ʃaɪn]	*briller*
ship	*(n.)*	[ʃɪp]	*navire*
shirt	*(n.)*	[ʃɜːt]	*chemise*
shoe	*(n.)*	[ʃuː]	*chaussure*
shoot	*(v. irrég.)*	[ʃuːt]	*tirer*
shooting	*(n.)*	[ʃuːtɪŋ]	*tir*
shop	*(n.)*	[ʃɒp]	*magasin*
shoulder	*(n.)*	['ʃəʊldəʳ]	*épaule*
shout	*(v.)*	[ʃaʊt]	*crier*
show	*(n.)*	[ʃəʊ]	*spectacle*
show	*(v. irrég.)*	[ʃəʊ]	*montrer*
shy	*(adj.)*	[ʃaɪ]	*timide*
sing	*(v. irrég.)*	[sɪŋ]	*chanter*
singer	*(n.)*	['sɪŋəʳ]	*chanteur*
sir	*(n.)*	[sɜːʳ]	*monsieur*
sister	*(n.)*	['sɪstəʳ]	*sœur*
sit sown	*(v. irrég.)*	[sɪt daʊn]	*s'asseoir*
skate	*(v.)*	[skeɪt]	*patiner*
skirt	*(n.)*	[skɜːt]	*jupe*
sleep	*(v. irrég.)*	[sliːp]	*dormir*
slide	*(v. irrég.)*	[slaɪd]	*glisser*
slow	*(adj.)*	[sləʊ]	*lent*
slowly	*(adv.)*	[sləʊlɪ]	*lentement*
small	*(adj.)*	[smɔːl]	*petit*
smart	*(adj.)*	[smɑːt]	*malin*
snake	*(n.)*	[sneɪk]	*serpent*
sneeze	*(v.)*	[sniːz]	*éternuer*
sock	*(n.)*	[sɒk]	*chaussette*
something	*(pron.)*	['sʌmθɪŋ]	*quelque chose*
sometimes	*(adv.)*	['sʌmtaɪmz]	*parfois*
son	*(n.)*	[sʌn]	*fils*
song	*(n.)*	[sɒŋ]	*chanson*
soon	*(adv.)*	[suːn]	*bientôt*
sorry	*(adj.)*	['sɒrɪ]	*désolé*
sound	*(n.)*	[saʊnd]	*son*
souvenir	*(n.)*	['suːvə'nɪəʳ]	*souvenir (achat)*
speak	*(v. irrég.)*	[spiːk]	*parler*
spell	*(v.)*	[spel]	*épeler*
spend	*(v. irrég.)*	[spend]	*passer (du temps)*
spider	*(n.)*	['spaɪdəʳ]	*araignée*
spinach	*(n.)*	['spɪnɪdʒ]	*épinard*
spot	*(v.)*	[spɒt]	*repérer*
spring	*(n.)*	[sprɪŋ]	*printemps*
stadium	*(n.)*	['steɪdɪəm]	*stade*
stage	*(n.)*	[steɪdʒ]	*scène de théatre*
stairs	*(n.)*	[stɛəz]	*escalier*
star	*(n.)*	[stɑːʳ]	*étoile / star*
stare	*(v.)*	[stɛəʳ]	*fixer avec attention*
start	*(v.)*	[stɑːt]	*commencer*
stay	*(v.)*	[steɪ]	*rester*
still	*(adv.)*	[stɪl]	*encore, toujours*
stone	*(n.)*	[stəʊn]	*pierre*
strange	*(adj.)*	[streɪndʒ]	*étrange*
street	*(n.)*	[striːt]	*rue*
strong	*(adj.)*	[strɒŋ]	*fort*
student	*(n.)*	['stjuːdənt]	*élève / étudiant*
study	*(n.)*	['stʌdɪ]	*bureau (pièce)*
subject	*(n.)*	['sʌbdʒɪkt]	*matière*

success	*(n.)*	[sək'ses]	*succès*
suit	*(n.)*	[su:t]	*costume*
summer	*(n.)*	['sʌməʳ]	*été*
sun	*(n.)*	[sʌn]	*soleil*
Sunday	*(n.)*	['sʌndeɪ]	*dimanche*
sunny	*(adj.)*	['sʌnɪ]	*ensoleillé*
supermarket	*(n.)*	['su:pəˌmɑ:kɪt]	*supermarché*
surprised	*(adj.)*	[sə'praɪzd]	*surpris*
surprising	*(adj.)*	[sə'praɪzɪŋ]	*surprenant*
sweet	*(adj.)*	[swi:t]	*doux, sucré*
sweet	*(n.)*	[swi:t]	*bonbon*
swim	*(v. irrég.)*	[swɪm]	*nager*
swimming	*(n.)*	['swɪmɪŋ]	*natation*
swimming-pool	*(n.)*	['swɪmɪŋ pu:l]	*piscine*
sword	*(n.)*	[sɔ:d]	*épée*

T

table	*(n.)*	['teɪbl]	*table*
take	*(v. irrég.)*	[teɪk]	*prendre*
take place	*(v. irrég.)*	[teɪk pleɪs]	*dérouler (se)*
talk	*(v.)*	[tɔ:k]	*converser*
tall	*(adj.)*	[tɔ:l]	*grand*
tea	*(n.)*	[ti:]	*thé*
teacher	*(n.)*	['ti:tʃəʳ]	*professeur*
team	*(n.)*	[ti:m]	*équipe*
team spirit	*(n.)*	[ti:m 'spɪrɪt]	*esprit d'équipe*
teddy bear	*(n.)*	['tedɪ beəʳ]	*ours en peluche*
tell	*(v. irrég.)*	[tel]	*dire, raconter*
text book	*(n.)*	['tekstbʊk]	*manuel scolaire*
thank	*(v.)*	[θæŋk]	*remercier*
thing	*(n.)*	[θɪŋ]	*chose*
think	*(v. irrég.)*	[θɪŋk]	*penser*
thirsty	*(adj.)*	['θɜ:stɪ]	*(be thirsty) avoir soif*
throw	*(vi.)*	[θrəʊ]	*jeter, lancer*
Thursday	*(n.)*	['θɜ:zdeɪ]	*jeudi*
tie	*(n.)*	[taɪ]	*cravate*
tights	*(n.)*	[taɪts]	*collants*
time	*(n.)*	[taɪm]	*heure*
timetable	*(n.)*	['taɪmteɪbl]	*emploi du temps*
today	*(adv.)*	[tə'deɪ]	*aujourd'hui*
toe	*(n.)*	[təʊ]	*doigt de pied*
toffee	*(n.)*	['tɒfɪ]	*caramel*
together	*(adv.)*	[tə'geðəʳ]	*ensemble*
tomato	*(n.)*	[tə'mɑ:təʊ]	*tomate*
tomb	*(n.)*	[tu:m]	*tombe*
tomorrow	*(adv.)*	[tə'mɒrəʊ]	*demain*
tonight	*(adv.)*	[tə'naɪt]	*ce soir*
top	*(n.)*	[tɒp]	*sommet*
touch	*(v.)*	[tʌtʃ]	*toucher*
tour	*(n.)*	['tʊəʳ]	*excursion*
tournament	*(n.)*	['tʊənəmənt]	*tournoi*
tower	*(n.)*	['taʊəʳ]	*tour*
tracksuit	*(n.)*	['træksu:t]	*survêtement*
train	*(v.)*	[treɪn]	*entraîner*
transform	*(v.)*	[træns'fɔm]	*transformer*
treasure	*(n.)*	['treʒəʳ]	*trésor*
treat	*(v.)*	[tri:t]	*traiter*
tree	*(n.)*	[tri:]	*arbre*
trousers	*(n.)*	['traʊzəz]	*pantalon*
true	*(adj.)*	[tru:]	*vrai*
try	*(v.)*	[traɪ]	*essayer*
try on	*(v.)*	[traɪ ɒn]	*essayer (un habit)*
Tuesday	*(n.)*	['tju:zdeɪ]	*mardi*
turn around	*(v.)*	[tɜ:n ə'raʊnd]	*se retourner*
turn left	*(v.)*	[tɜ:n left]	*tourner à gauche*
turn on/off	*(v.)*	[tɜ:n ɒn ɒf]	*allumer / éteindre*
turn right	*(v.)*	[tɜ:n raɪt]	*tourner à droite*
TV show	*(n.)*	['ti:'vi: ʃəʊ]	*émission de télé*

U

ugly	*(adj.)*	['ʌglɪ]	*laid*
uncle	*(n.)*	['ʌŋkl]	*oncle*
under	*(prép.)*	['ʌndəʳ]	*sous*
understand	*(v. irrég.)*	[ˌʌndə'stænd]	*comprendre*
unfortunately	*(adv.)*	[ʌn'fɔ:tʃənɪtlɪ]	*malheureusement*
uniform	*(n.)*	['ju:nifɔ:m]	*uniforme*
upstairs	*(adv.)*	[ʌp'stɛəz]	*en haut*
use	*(v.)*	[ju:z]	*utiliser*
usually	*(adv.)*	['ju:ʒʊəlɪ]	*habituellement*

V

vegetables	*(n.)*	['vedʒtəbls]	*légumes*
vegetarian	*(n.)*	['vedʒɪ'tɛərɪən]	*végétarien*
versus	*(prép.)*	['vɜ:səs]	*contre*
very	*(adv.)*	['verɪ]	*très*
victory	*(n.)*	['vɪktərɪ]	*victoire*
visit	*(v.)*	['vɪzɪt]	*visiter, rendre visite*
visitor	*(n.)*	['vɪzɪtəʳ]	*visiteur*

W

wait	*(v.)*	[weɪt]	*attendre*
wake up	*(v. irrég.)*	[weɪk ʌp]	*se réveiller*
walk	*(v.)*	[wɔ:k]	*marcher*
wall	*(n.)*	[wɔ:l]	*mur*
want	*(v.)*	[wɒnt]	*vouloir*
wash	*(v.)*	[wɒʃ]	*laver*
watch	*(v.)*	[wɒtʃ]	*regarder*
water	*(n.)*	['wɔ:təʳ]	*eau*
way	*(n.)*	[weɪ]	*chemin*
wear	*(v. irrég.)*	[wɛəʳ]	*porter (sur soi)*
Wednesday	*(n.)*	['wenzdeɪ]	*mercredi*
week	*(n.)*	[wi:k]	*semaine*
weekend	*(n.)*	['wi:k'end]	*fin de semaine*
welcome	*(v.)*	['welkəm]	*accueillir*
well	*(adv.)*	[wel]	*bien*
Welsh	*(adj.)*	[welʃ]	*gallois*
what	*(pron.)*	[wɒt]	*que, quoi, quel*
what time	*(pron.)*	[wɒt taɪm]	*quelle heure*
when	*(pron.)*	[wen]	*quand*
where	*(pron.)*	[wɛəʳ]	*où*
white	*(adj.)*	[waɪt]	*blanc*
who	*(pron.)*	[hu:]	*qui*
whose	*(pron.)*	[hu:z]	*à qui*
why	*(pron.)*	[waɪ]	*pourquoi*
win	*(v. irrég.)*	[wɪn]	*gagner*
window	*(n.)*	['wɪndəʊ]	*fenêtre*
wine	*(n.)*	[waɪn]	*vin*
winter	*(n.)*	['wɪntəʳ]	*hiver*
with	*(prép.)*	[wɪð]	*avec*
wood	*(n.)*	[wʊd]	*bois / forêt*
word	*(n.)*	[wɜ:d]	*mot*
work	*(v.)*	[wɜ:k]	*travailler*
worse	*(adj.)*	[wɜ:s]	*pire*
worst	*(adj.)*	[wɜ:st]	*le pire*
write	*(v. irrég.)*	[raɪt]	*écrire*

Y

year	*(n.)*	[jɪəʳ]	*an, année*
year 7	*(n.)*	[jɪəʳ'sevn]	*classe de sixième*
yellow	*(adj.)*	['jeləʊ]	*jaune*
yesterday	*(adv.)*	['jestədeɪ]	*hier*
young	*(adj.)*	[jʌŋ]	*jeune*
yucky!	*(onomat.)*	['jʌkɪ]	*beurk!*
yummy!	*(onomat.)*	['jʌmɪ]	*miam miam!*

Lexique français-anglais

Ce lexique t'aidera pour faire toutes les activités du manuel.

A

à côté de	*next to, near*
à droite	*on the right*
à gauche	*on the left*
accueillir	*welcome*
acheter	*buy (v. irrég. bought)*
acteur	*actor*
actrice	*actress*
aéroport	*airport*
agence de voyage	*travel agency*
agent de voyage	*travel agent*
agressif	*aggressive*
aider	*help*
aimer	*like, love*
aller	*go (v. irrég. went)*
aller tout droit	*go straight (v. irrég. went straight)*
américain	*American*
ami	*friend*
amuser (s')	*have fun (v. irrég. had fun)*
anglais	*English*
animal domestique	*pet*
appeler	*call*
après	*after*
après-midi	*afternoon*
araignée	*spider*
arbitre	*referee*
arbre	*tree*
arc-en-ciel	*rainbow*
argent	*money*
arriver	*arrive*
assiette	*plate*
attraper	*catch (v. irrég. caught)*
australien	*Australian*
autocar	*coach*
automne	*autumn*
avion	*airplane*
avoir faim	*be hungry (v. irrég. was hungry)*
avoir soif	*be thirsty (v. irrég. was thirsty)*

B

bague	*ring*
bateau	*boat*
battre	*beat (v. irrég. beat)*
beau	*beautiful*
bio	*organic*
blanc	*white*
bleu	*blue*
bœuf	*beef*
boire	*drink (v. irrég. drank)*
boîte	*box*
bon	*good*
bonbon	*sweet*
boucherie	*butcher's*
boulangerie	*bakery*
bras	*arm*
britannique	*British*
bureau	*desk*
bus	*bus*
but	*goal*

C

café	*café, pub*
cahier	*copybook*
calme	*quiet*
campagne	*countryside*
carotte	*carrot*
carpet	*tapis*
cartable	*school bag*
carte	*map*
casquette	*cap*
casser	*break (v. irrég. broke)*
cathédrale	*cathedral*
ceinture	*belt*
célèbre	*famous*
chaise	*chair*
chambre	*bedroom*
chanter	*sing (v. irrég. sang)*
chanteur	*singer*
chapeau	*hat*
chaque	*every*
chat	*cat*
château	*castle*
chaussettes	*socks*
chaussures	*shoes*
chemin	*way*
cheminée	*fireplace*
chemise	*shirt*
cher	*expensive*
cher (dans une lettre)	*dear*
chien	*dog*
chips	*crisps*
chocolat	*chocolate*
chose	*thing*
cinéma	*cinema*
circuit touristique	*tour*
cirque	*circus*
clé	*key*
client	*customer*
coca	*Coke*
colline	*hill*
combien	*how much, how many*
comédie musicale	*musical*
commencer	*start, begin (v. irrég. began)*
comment	*how*
conduire	*drive (v. irrég. drove)*
confiant	*confident*
confortable	*comfortable, cosy*
conte	*tale*
content	*happy*
corbeau	*raven*
costume	*suit*
costume (de théatre)	*costume*
coucher (se)	*go to bed (v. irrég. went to bed)*
couleur	*colour*
cour de récréation	*playground*
courageux	*brave*
courir	*run (v. irrég. ran)*
couronne	*crown*
course	*race*
courses (faire des)	*go shopping (v. irrég. went shopping)*
cousin	*cousin*
cravate	*tie*
crayon	*pencil*
cuisine	*kitchen*
cuisiner	*cook*

D

dans	*in*
danse	*dance*
danser	*dance*
déçu	*disappointed*
défaite	*defeat*
défilé de mode	*fashion show*
défiler	*parade*
déjeuner	*lunch*
demain	*tomorrow*
derrière	*behind*
désolé	*sorry*
dessiner	*draw (v. irrég. drew)*
détenir	*hold (v. irrég. held)*

devant	*in front of*
devenir	*become (v. irrég. became)*
deviner	*guess*
difficile	*difficult*
dîner	*dinner*
dire	*say, tell (v. irrég. said, told)*
divorcer	*divorce*
doigt	*finger*
donc	*so*
donner	*give (v. irrég. gave)*
donner un coup de pied	*kick*
dormir	*sleep (v. irrég. slept)*
droite (la)	*right*
drôle	*funny*

E

eau	*water*
écossais	*Scottish*
écouter	*listen to*
écraser	*crush*
écrire	*write (v. irrég. wrote)*
effrayé	*scared*
église	*church*
élève	*pupil*
embarrassé	*embarrassed*
emmener	*take (v. irrég. took)*
emploi du temps	*timetable*
en bas	*downstairs*
en colère	*angry*
en dessous	*under*
en haut	*upstairs*
en retard	*late*
enthousiaste	*excited*
ensemble	*together*
ensuite	*then*
entendre	*hear (v. irrég. heard)*
entraîneur	*coach*
entre	*between*
entrer	*come in (v. irrég. came in)*
épaule	*shoulder*
épée	*sword*
épeler	*spell (v. irrég. spelt)*
équipe	*team*
escalier	*stairs*
essayer (un vêtement)	*try on*
et	*and*
étagère	*shelf*
été	*summer*
étrange	*strange*
excursion	*tour*
expliquer	*explain*
explorer	*explore*
extérieur (à l')	*outside*

F

facile	*easy*
famille	*family*
fantôme	*ghost*
fascinant	*fascinating*
faux	*false*
fée	*fairy*
félicitations	*congratulations*
fenêtre	*window*
ferme	*farm*
fermer	*close*
fêtes	*celebrations*
fête	*party*
fêter	*celebrate*
fiancer (se)	*get engaged (v. irrég. got engaged)*
film	*film, movie*
finalement	*finally*
flèche	*arrow*
forêt	*forest*
fort	*strong*
fou	*crazy*
français	*French*
frapper	*hit (v. irrég. hit)*
frère	*brother*
frites	*chips*
fromage	*cheese*
fruit	*fruit*

G

gagner	*win (v. irrég. won)*
garage	*garage*
gare	*train station*
gâteau	*cake*
gauche	*left*
genou	*knee*
gentil	*nice*
glace	*ice-cream*
gomme	*eraser*
grand	*tall, large*
grand-mère	*grandmother*
grand-père	*grandfather*
grenier	*attic*
gris	*grey*
gros	*big*
grotte	*cave*
guide	*guide*
guitare	*guitar*

H

habiller (s')	*get dressed (v. irrég. got dressed)*
habiter	*live*
hamster	*hamster*
haricot	*bean*
heureusement	*fortunately*
hier	*yesterday*
hiver	*winter*
horloge	*clock*
hôtel	*hotel*
hourrah	*hurray*

I

idiot	*stupid*
île	*island*
imperméable	*raincoat*
impressionné	*impressed*
incroyable	*incredible*
intelligent	*clever*
intéressant	*interesting*
intérieur (à l')	*inside*
inviter	*invite*
itinéraire	*itinerary, tour*

J

jamais	*never*
jambe	*leg*
jambon	*ham*
jardin	*garden*
jaune	*yellow*
jeter	*throw (v. irrég. threw)*
jeu vidéo	*video game*
jeune	*young*
joli	*pretty*
jouer	*play*
jouer (au théâtre)	*act*
joueur	*player*
journée, jour	*day*
jupe	*skirt*
jus de fruit	*fruit juice*

L

lac	*lake*
lait	*milk*
lapin	*rabbit*
laver	*wash*
légume	*vegetable*
lent	*slow*
lever (se)	*get up (v. irrég. got up)*
librairie	*bookshop*
lire	*read (v. irrég. read)*
lit	*bed*
loisir	*hobby*
louer	*rent*
lunettes	*glasses*
lutin	*lutin, elf*

Lexique français-anglais

M

magasin	*shop*
main	*hand*
mais	*but*
maison	*house*
maladroit	*clumsy*
manger	*eat (v. irrég. ate)*
mannequin	*model*
marcher	*walk*
marier (se)	*get married (v. irrég. got married)*
marquer	*score*
marraine	*godmother*
matière	*subject*
mauvais	*bad*
mémoire	*memory*
mer	*sea*
mère	*mother*
metteur en scène	*director*
mettre	*put (v. irrég. put)*
mettre sur soi	*put on (v. irrég. put on)*
midi	*noon*
mince	*thin*
minuit	*midnight*
mode	*fashion*
mois	*month*
monstre	*monster*
montagne	*mountain*
monter à (faire du) vélo	*ride (v. irrég. rode)*
monument	*monument*
moto	*motorbike*
mourir	*die*
mur	*wall*
musique	*music*

N

nager	*swim (v. irrég. swam)*
naître	*be born (v. irrég. was born)*
natation	*swimming*
nationalité	*nationality*
navire	*ship*
neveu	*nephew*
nez	*nose*
nièce	*niece*
noir	*black*
nom	*name*
nourriture	*food*
nuage	*cloud*
nuit	*night*

O

oeil	*eye*
oeuf	*egg*
oiseau	*bird*
oncle	*uncle*
ordinateur	*computer*
oreille	*ear*
organiser	*organize*
ou	*or*
où	*where*
oublier	*forget (v. irrég. forgot)*
ouvrir	*open*

P

panier	*basket*
panneau	*sign*
pantalon	*trousers*
parapluie	*umbrella*
parce que	*because*
parfois	*sometimes*
parler	*speak (v. irrég. spoke)*
partout	*everywhere*
passer (se)	*take place, happen (v. irrég. took place)*
pays	*country*
paysage	*landscape*
penser	*think (v. irrég. thought)*
perdre	*lose (v. irrég. lost)*
père	*father*
petit	*small, little, short*
petit ami	*boyfriend*
petit déjeuner	*breakfast*
petite amie	*girlfriend*
phrase	*sentence*
piano	*piano*
pièce	*room*
pièce de théatre	*play*
pied	*foot, feet (pl)*
pierre	*stone*
piscine	*swimming-pool*
plafond	*ceiling*
poisson	*fish*
pomme de terre	*potato*
port	*harbour*
porte	*door*
porter sur soi	*wear (v. irrég. wore)*
poste	*post office*
poubelle	*bin*
poulet	*chicken*
pourquoi	*why*
préféré	*favourite*
préférer	*prefer*
prendre	*take (v. irrég. took)*
prénom	*first name*
prétentieux	*pretentious*
principal	*headmaster*
printemps	*spring*
prix	*price*
prochain	*next*
professeur	*teacher*
public (le)	*audience*

Q

que, quel	*what*
quel âge	*how old*
qui	*who*

R

rapide	*fast*
record	*record*
regarder	*watch, look at*
règle	*ruler*
reine	*queen*
rencontrer	*meet (v. irrég. met)*
répéter	*repeat*
répondre	*answer*
restaurant	*restaurant*
rester	*stay*
réveiller (se)	*wake up (v. irrég. woke up)*
rêver	*dream (v. irrég. dreamed ou dreamt)*
rien	*nothing*
rivière	*river*
robe	*dress*
roi	*king*
rôle	*part*
rose	*pink*
rouge	*red*

S

sac d'école	*school bag*
saison	*season*
salade	*salad*
salle à manger	*dining-room*
salle de bain	*bathroom*
salle de classe	*classroom*
salon	*living-room*
santé	*health*
saucisse	*sausage*
sauter	*jump*

savoir	*know (v. irrég. knew)*
scène	*scene*
scène (de théatre)	*stage*
séduisant	*attractive*
semaine	*week*
sentiment	*feeling*
seulement	*only*
sixième	*year 7*
sœur	*sister*
sol d'un bâtiment	*floor*
soleil	*sun*
sombre	*dark*
soupe	*soup*
sous-vêtements	*underwear*
souvenir (se)	*remember*
souvent	*often*
spectacle	*show*
sportif	*sportsman*
sportif (adj.)	*athletic*
stade	*stadium*
studieux	*hard-working*
stylo	*pen*
super	*great*
supermarché	*supermarket*
sur	*on*
surnom	*nickname*
surprenant	*amazing*
surpris	*surprised*
sympa	*cool*

T

table	*table*
tableau	*painting*
tante	*aunt*
tasse	*cup, mug*
téléphone	*phone*
téléphone portable	*mobile phone*
terrain de football	*football camp*
tête	*head*
thé	*tea*
timide	*shy*
tir à l'arc	*archery*
tirer	*shoot (v. irrég. shot)*
tomate	*tomato*
tombe	*tomb, grave*
tomber	*fall (v. irrég. fell)*
toucher	*touch*
toujours	*always*
tour	*tower*
touriste	*tourist*
tourner	*turn*
tournoi	*tournament*
tout d'abord	*first*
train	*train*
travailler	*work*
traverser	*cross*
triste	*sad*
trotinette	*scooter*
trousse	*pencil-case*
trouver	*find (v. irrég. found)*
tuer	*kill*

U

uniforme	*uniform*
utiliser	*use*

V

vélo	*bike, bicycle*
venir	*come (v. irrég. came)*
vert	*green*
veste	*jacket*
vêtements	*clothes*
viande	*meat*
victoire	*victory*
vie	*life*
vieux	*old*
village	*village*
ville	*town, city*
visage	*face*
visiter	*visit*
vite	*quick*
vivre	*live*
voir	*see (v. irrég. saw)*
voiture	*car*
voler	*fly (v. irrég. flew)*
vouloir	*want*
voyage	*trip*
voyager	*travel*
vrai	*true*

Crédits photographiques

Couverture : hg : Orédia/Sébastien Godere ; **hd :** Shutterstock/Ken McDougall ; **mhd :** Getty/Image Bank/Geoffrey Clifford ; **mbg :** Corbis/Destinations ; **bg :** Shutterstock/Tatiana Popova ; **bd :** Rea/Report Digital/Paul Box

11h : Shutterstock/J.-E. Rozey ; **11b :** Shutterstock/A. Shankweiler ; **17 :** Education Photos/John Walmsley ; **20 :** Marie Alix Cazalaa ; **23 :** Education Photos/John Walmsley ; **26g :** Getty/Image Bank/Peter Adams ; **26hd :** AFP/Koichi Kamoshida ; **26md :** Eyedea/Hoa Qui/Wojtek Buss ; **26b :** Marie Alix Cazalaa ; **29g :** Rue des Archives/BCA ; **29d :** Rue des Archives/BCA ; **30 :** Education Photos/John Walmsley ; **31h :** Education Photos/John Walmsley ; **31bg :** Education Photos/John Walmsley ; **31bd :** Istock/Brett Mulcahy ; **33 :** Bree Anne Buckley ; **36 :** Marie Alix Cazalaa ; **39 :** Corbis/Lisa B. ; **42 :** Getty/Photographer's Choice/Peter Dazeley ; **46hg :** Corbis/Design Pics/Colleen Cahill ; **46mg :** Corbis/Edifice ; **46md :** Corbis/Edifice/Philippa Lewis ; **46b :** Getty/Stockfood/Miki Duisterhof ; **47g :** Sucré Salé/Lippman ; **47d :** Rea/Report Digital/Paul Box ; **49 :** Abaca Press/PA Archives/John Stillwell ; **51g :** Corbis/Eurasia Press/Steven Vilder ; **51d :** Eyedea/Gamma/Alain Benainous ; **52 :** Photo12.com/Alamy/John Carter ; **55 :** Getty/Taxi/Paul Windsor ; **58 :** Photo12.com/Alamy/Roger Crackwell ; **62h :** Getty/DEA/A. Dagli Orti ; **62b :** Photononstop/Eurasia Press ; **63hg :** Eyedea/Rapho/Emile Luider ; **63hd :** Eyedea/Image State/Steve Vidler ; **63b :** Shutterstock/R. Nagy ; **65 :** Corbis/Eleanor Brentall ; **68 :** Getty/Image Bank/Paul Viant ; **71 :** Age/Travelpix/Steve Vidler ; **74 :** Photo12.com/Alamy/Realimage ; **77 :** Getty/Iconica/Peter Cade ; **83 :** Photononstop/Eurasia Press ; **84h :** Getty/Time & Life Images/Ken Goff ; **84m :** Sipa/Rex Features ; **84b :** Eyedea/Gamma/Ian Jones ; **85hg :** Eyedea/Gamma/Ian Jones ; **85hd :** Eyedea/Gamma/KPA ; **85b :** Eyedea/Camera Press/Glenn Harvey ; **87 :** Cit'en scène/Pacome Poirier ; **88mg et d :** Coll. Christophe L ; **88md :** Rue des Archives/Snap Photo ; **88bd :** Coll. Christophe L ; **90hg :** Coll. Christophe L ; **90hm :** Coll. Christophe L ; **90hd :** Rue des Archives/BCA ; **90b :** Education Photos/John Walmsley ; **91 :** Coll. Christophe L ; **93 :** Getty/Jupiterimages/Workbook Stock ; **94g :** Eyedea/Gamma/Tsuni ; **94mg :** Eyedea/UPI/David Silpa ; **94md :** Eyedea/Celebrity/Gilbert Flores ; **94d :** Sipa/AP/Kevork Djansezian ; **99 :** Coll. Christophe L ; **100hd :** Eyedea/Celebrity/Rusty ; **100bg :** Corbis/Bettmann ; **100bmg :** Rue des Archives/BCA ; **100bmd :** Eyedea/Gamma/Benainous-Lefranc ; **100bd :** Rue des Archives/RDA ; **102 :** Coll. Christophe L ; **106hg :** Age/Kord.com ; **106hd :** The Kobal Collection/Warner Bros ; **106m :** Coll. Christophe L ; **106bg :** Coll. Christophe L ; **106bd :** Rue des Archives/BCA ; **107hg :** Coll. Christophe L ; **107hd :** Coll. Christophe L ; **107b :** Coll. Christophe L ; **109 :** Shutterstock/James Blinn ; **110hg :** Rea/Pierre Gleizes ; **110hm :** Istock/Brian Kelly ; **110hd :** Hémis.fr/René Mattes ; **110bg :** Adrian Pingstone ; **110bm :** Hémis.fr/René Mattes ; **110bd :** Corbis/Destinations ; **112hg :** Hémis.fr/Patrick Frilet ; **112hm :** Corbis/Hein van Den Heuvel ; **112hd :** Age/The Irish Image Collection ; **112mg :** Age/Wojtek Buss ; **112mm :** Age/Index Stock/Jacob Halaska ; **112md :** Hémis.fr/Bertrand Rieger ; **112b :** Photo12.com/Alamy/Peter Forsberg ; **115 :** Age/The Irish Image Collection ; **116 :** AFP/Getty/Chris Jackson ; **118hg :** Eyedea/Gamma/Benainous-Duclos ; **118hm :** Eyedea/Gamma/KPA ; **118hd :** Eyedea/UPI/David Silpa ; **118bg :** Bridgeman-Giraudon ; **118bmg :** Bridgeman-Giraudon/British Library Board ; **118bmd :** Bridgeman-Giraudon ; **118bd :** Bridgeman-Giraudon ; **121 :** Eyedea/KPA/Robert Marquardt ; **122hg :** Shutterstock/Vospalej ; **122mhg :** Getty/Riser/Laurence Monneret ; **122hd :** Age/The Irish Image Collection ; **122m :** Sipa/Superstock ; **122b :** Corbis/Design Pics/David L. Brown ; **123h :** AFP/Peter Muhly ; **123b :** Corbis/Destinations ; **125 :** Getty/Stone/Alexander Hubrich ; **128 :** Action Plus/Glyn Kirk ; **131 :** Presse-Sports/Offside/Simon Stacpoole ; **134g :** AFP/Robyn Beck ; **134d :** Corbis/Transtock/David Freers ; **137 :** Presse-Sports/Offside/Simon Stacpoole ; **138hg :** Sipa/AP/Jane Mingay ; **138mh :** Uma Press/Giuliano Belavicqua ; **138md :** Action Plus ; **138b :** Action Plus/Neil Egerton ; **139g :** Reuters/Tobt Melville ; **139hd :** Action Plus/Glyn Kirk ; **139bd :** AFP/Adrian Dennis ; **140hg :** Corbis/Ed Bock ; **140hd :** Getty/Photodisc/Kevin Laubacher ; **140bg :** Getty/Dorling Kindersley/Andy Crawford ; **140bmg :** Corbis/Moodboard ; **140bmd :** Shutterstock/Carlo Dapino ; **140bd :** Shutterstock/Paul B. Moore ; **141h :** Shutterstock/E. Starshaya ; **141b :** Corbis/Lew Robertson ; **141m :** Sucré Salé/J. Bilic ; **142h :** Bridgeman-Giraudon/Philip Mould Ltd ; **142m :** Bridgeman-Giraudon ; **142b :** Bridgeman-Giraudon/The Stapleton Collection ; **143h :** Photolibrary/Britain on View ; **143b :** Photo12.com/Alamy/Homer Sykes ; **144hg :** Photononstop/Mauritius/Matthias Tunger ; **144hd :** Corbis/Sofood/Hussenot ; **144bg :** Shutterstock/Vnlit ; **144bd :** Shutterstock/Godrick ; **145hg :** Age/Superstock ; **145hd :** Getty/Dorling Kindersley/Andy Crawford ; **145b :** Shutterstock/Pdesign ; **146h :** Getty/New York Daily News ; **146m :** AFP/Thimothy A. Clary ; **146b :** Photo12.com/Alamy/Frances Roberts ; **147h :** Istock/Jack Puccio ; **147bg :** Sipa/AP/Jim Barcus ; **147bd :** Getty/New York Daily News ; **148 :** Coll. Christophe L ; **158 :** Age/Prisma/Steve Vidler ; **159 :** Corbis/Skyscan

Crédit texte: p. 148-149 : Black Cat Publishing, an imprint of Cideb Editrice, Genoa, Canterbury

N° d'éditeur 10171627 - Dépôt légal : Juillet 2010
Imprimé en France par MAURY

GREAT BRITAIN AND IRELAND
The British Isles
The United Kingdom
Great Britain
ATLANTIC OCEAN
North Sea
Irish Sea
SCOTLAND
Inverness
Aberdeen
Dundee
Perth
Glasgow
Edinburgh
NORTHERN IRELAND (ULSTER)
Belfast
REPUBLIC OF IRELAND (EIRE)
Dublin
Tyne
Newcastle-upon-Tyne
York
Leeds
Hull
Liverpool
Manchester
Sheffield
Trent
Nottingham
Leicester
Norwich
Birmingham
Severn
Cambridge
WALES
Stratford-upon-Avon
Swansea
Oxford
ENGLAND
London
Bristol
Cardiff
Bath
Thames
Canterbury
Channel Tunnel
Dover
Calais
BELGI
ATLANTIC OCEAN
Southampton
Portsmouth
Brighton
Boulogne-sur-Mer
Plymouth
Isle of Wight
The English Channel
FRANCE
Le Havre
100 km

THE ENGLISH-SPEAKING WORLD